Cambridge Elements ≡

Elements in Political Economy
edited by
David Stasavage
New York University

THE ECONOMIC ORIGINS OF POLITICAL PARTIES

Christopher Kam
University of British Columbia

Adlai Newson
University of British Columbia

CAMBRIDGE
UNIVERSITY PRESS

CAMBRIDGE
UNIVERSITY PRESS

University Printing House, Cambridge CB2 8BS, United Kingdom

One Liberty Plaza, 20th Floor, New York, NY 10006, USA

477 Williamstown Road, Port Melbourne, VIC 3207, Australia

314–321, 3rd Floor, Plot 3, Splendor Forum, Jasola District Centre, New Delhi – 110025, India

79 Anson Road, #06–04/06, Singapore 079906

Cambridge University Press is part of the University of Cambridge.

It furthers the University's mission by disseminating knowledge in the pursuit of education, learning, and research at the highest international levels of excellence.

www.cambridge.org
Information on this title: www.cambridge.org/9781108828420
DOI: 10.1017/9781108908726

First published 2020

A catalogue record for this publication is available from the British Library.

ISBN 978-1-108-82842-0 Paperback
ISSN 2398-4031 (online)
ISSN 2514-3816 (print)

The Economic Origins of Political Parties

Elements in Political Economy

DOI: 10.1017/9781108908726
Firstpublishedonline: November 2020

Christopher Kam
University of British Columbia

Adlai Newson
University of British Columbia

Author for correspondence: Christopher Kam, chris.kam@ubc.ca

Abstract: This Element examines how the changing economic basis of parliamentary elections in nineteenth-century England and Wales contributed to the development of modern parties and elections. Even after the 1832 Reform Act expanded the British electorate, elections in many constituencies went uncontested, party labels were nominal, and candidates spent large sums treating and bribing voters. By the end of the century, however, almost every constituency was contested, candidates stood as representatives of national parties, and campaigns were fought on the basis of policies. We show how industrialization, the spread of literacy, and the rise of cheap newspapers encouraged candidates to enter and contest constituencies. The increased expense that came from fighting frequent elections in larger constituencies induced copartisan candidates to form slates. This imparted a uniform partisan character to parliamentary elections that facilitated the emergence of programmatic political parties.

Keywords: political parties, elections, modernization theory, economics, literacy

ISBNs: 9781108828420 (PB), 9781108908726 (OC)
ISSNs: 2398-4031 (online), 2514-3816 (print)

Contents

1 Introduction

One can break England's path to political modernization into three phases. In the first phase, prior to the First Reform Act of 1832, electoral competition in many constituencies was stifled by aristocratic families or cliques of town officials who controlled the conduct and outcome of elections. The second phase, bookended by the First and Second (1867) Reform Acts, saw many constituencies open up to electoral competition. The spread of electoral contestation was not uniform, however. Where elections took place candidates styled themselves as Liberals or Conservatives, but they tended to compete independently, and they often spent large sums to treat and bribe voters. Elections hinged as much on the amounts the candidates spent as on their party labels. In the final phase that followed the Second Reform Act, parliamentary elections and political parties began to take on their modern form, with candidates contesting constituencies as representatives of national parties with defined policy positions. This process was completed with the passage of the Third Reform Act (1884). Change thus proceeded on three dimensions: elections became increasingly competitive; they were increasingly national and partisan in character; and they were increasingly programmatic.

This Element examines the mechanisms that facilitated the emergence, homogenization, and nationalization of electoral competition. Lipset and Rokkan (1967) referred to this evolution as a process of *local entrenchment*, by which they meant the process by which local party organizations defined the set of political alternatives available to local electorates. The nationalization of such local efforts was crucial to the development of modern electoral democracy because it provided voters across a country with a meaningful choice over a common set of party labels and infused those labels with shared meaning (Caramani 2004; Chhibber and Kollman 2004; Hicken 2009). Programmatic politics cannot operate in the absence of such conditions. Indeed, this was the conclusion of Key's (1949) classic comparison of party systems and politics in the Northern and Southern US states. The problem that Key diagnosed in the Southern states was not simply a lack of competition between parties, but that in the absence of such competition, parties never developed beyond a set of transitory factions that by their nature could neither transmit nor receive programmatic demands.

This Element is driven by two questions:

1. What made candidates increasingly willing to contest parliamentary elections, especially in constituencies that had hitherto been uncompetitive?
2. What induced candidates to abandon the old tradition of campaigning independently and to instead contest elections as party standard-bearers?

The answers to these questions, we argue, reside in the changing economic basis of nineteenth-century parliamentary election campaigns. By "economic basis" we mean not only the average and marginal costs involved in mounting election campaigns, but also the socioeconomic context in which these campaigns took place and the collective action problems that candidates confronted in organizing them.

Implicit in our economic perspective on candidates, parties, and elections is the assumption that political parties are organizations that are crafted to win elections; ideological appeals are a means to this end and not an end in themselves (Downs 1957; Schlesinger 1984). This does not imply that ideology plays no role in building and maintaining a political party. Our position is, rather, that some of the important collective action problems that party members confront are not ideological but economic in nature, and that shared ideology is by itself insufficient to resolve these economic collective action problems.

For Lipset and Rokkan, as for many other scholars (e.g., Ostrogorski 1902; Duverger 1962; LaPalombara and Weiner 1966), it was the extension of the franchise that spurred the emergence of local party organizations and the adoption of programmatic appeals. An enlarged electorate generated significant electoral advantages to those capable of mobilizing and coordinating voters (Salmon 2002). Moreover, as long as elections were based on the delivery of private goods to individual voters, candidates' electioneering costs increased with the size of the electorate. By contrast, programmatic appeals based on the delivery of public goods promised candidates significant economies of scale in the context of a mass electorate (Kitschelt and Wilkinson 2007; Stokes et al. 2013). The greater efficiency of programmatic electoral strategies relative to clientelistic electoral strategies led to the former displacing the latter.

This standard account of the transition from clientelistic to programmatic electoral competition is parsimonious. It is also consistent with the fact that programmatic electoral competition in England (and many other countries besides) tended to arrive with the extension of the suffrage. The account is not without difficulties, however. First, the economies of scale that presumably make programmatic appeals the superior electoral strategy are realized in the context of competitive elections (Kitschelt and Wilkinson 2007, 7, 29). However, throughout much of the period we are concerned with, the existence of electoral contestation cannot be taken as given (Caramani 2003; Gash 1953; Lloyd 1965). The question of the pace and extent to which electoral contestation took hold at nineteenth-century parliamentary elections is thus central to understanding the rise of programmatic politics in England.

Second, the coherence and credibility of programmatic appeals requires candidates of the same party to agree on a program (Kitschelt and Wilkinson

2007, 9). How party members come to agree on this program is one of the central collective action problems that political parties confront (Aldrich 1995; Schlesinger 1984) – but it is not the only one. Programmatic electoral strategies may be more efficient than clientelistic strategies, but they are not free; advertising and voter mobilization, for example, always required significant amounts of money. In the modern era, it is usually the case that central party organizations possess the administrative and financial capacity to produce and distribute campaign resources to local candidates. This was not so in Victorian England.

The central party organizations (such as they were) on both the Liberal and Conservative sides did not become administratively autonomous – in the sense that their continuity and efficacy was independent of the energy and competence of one or two particular people – until the early 1870s (Hanham 1959; Rix 2016). Hence, for much of the period that we are concerned with, there was no central party organization to assign candidates to constituencies, to coordinate the efforts of copartisan candidates, or to fund local campaigns; this was only gradually and fitfully built up over the course of the nineteenth century (Gwynn 1962; Gash 1983; Jaggard 2008; Newbould 1985).

On the contrary, the expectation was for candidates to provide their own campaign funding (Gash 1953, 112, 134–135; Hanham 1959). A candidate's ability to bear their own expenses and, on winning, to financially sustain their electoral interest in the constituency demonstrated "independence." Independence was a prized quality in a candidate; it implied disinterest, whereas partisanship implied self-interest. This normative stance reflected a traditional understanding of parties as instruments of faction rather than representation (Scarrow 2006). As an organizational principle, however, the financial imbalance between the central parties and their candidates had two important implications. First, party leaders could not dictate when and where elections would be contested: that depended on the candidates themselves being willing to undertake the expense of a contested election. Second, in the double-member constituencies that were typical of the nineteenth-century English electoral system, the expectation that each candidate would provide his own funds created a financial free-rider problem: copartisans were reluctant to contribute financially to a united Liberal or Conservative campaign absent some assurance that their contribution would work to get themselves, and not just their running mate, elected. Again, the organizational and financial weakness of the central parties meant that party leaders lacked the means to compel their own candidates to cooperate at elections.

We thus arrive at a puzzle. Programmatic electoral strategies drive out clientelistic electoral strategies, but only under the pressures of electoral competition. Contested elections, even if run along programmatic lines, remain expensive, however. The candidates who paid these expenses were understandably reluctant to fight elections unless their prospects of victory were good – but such prospects cannot be good for all candidates in all constituencies. This stunted electoral contestation. Furthermore, even when elections were contested, candidates in double-member constituencies were wary of financial free-riding by their fellow copartisans. This stunted the emergence of party slates. In consequence, electoral competition continued to run along parochial and personal lines rather than along national and partisan lines.

1.1 Argument

How, then, did electoral contestation emerge? And how did copartisan candidates in multimember constituencies overcome their financial free-riding problems and begin to fight elections as party slates? Our answers to these questions begin with the assumption that candidates contested elections only in constituencies where their marginal benefits exceeded their marginal costs. If the marginal benefit of a contested election to a candidate increased with the candidate's probability of winning a seat, then, all else being equal, candidates should contest elections in constituencies where their probabilities of winning are high and avoid elections in constituencies where they are low. A contested election occurs when and where the number of candidates who judge their probability of winning a seat to be sufficiently high exceeds the number of seats on offer.

The probability of the candidate of a given party winning a seat was strongly correlated with the structure of the constituency. The politics of the era was defined by two social cleavages: one involving economics, the other, religion (Jaggard 2004; Phillips 1992). The Conservatives positioned themselves as the defenders of the Church of England, but even more so, the party of agriculture (Adelman 1989, 90; Aydelotte 1966). The Liberals were, in contrast, the party of nonconformism and industry. Accordingly, Conservatives tended to perform well in the counties and smaller boroughs where agricultural interests were predominant, whereas Liberals were more likely to win elections in industrial cities and towns with significant nonconformist communities. These expectations meant that elections were contested in constituencies where patterns of land ownership, economic production, and religious affiliation presented candidates of both parties with reasonable prospects of victory. Conversely, constituencies where such factors overwhelmingly favored the electoral success of one party were unlikely to be contested by candidates of the opposing party.

We label the degree to which the balance of social cleavages in a given constituency favored the election of one party's candidates over the others as the *structural bias* of the party system. The structural bias of the party system at the start of the period advantaged the Conservatives.[1] While industry had eclipsed agriculture as the main driver of the English economy by 1832, the agricultural sector remained sizable, and its interests were protected by the disproportionate parliamentary representation of small provincial boroughs that were dependent on the agricultural economy of their surrounding counties (Seymour 1915). The religious interests of the Church of England needed no such protection: more than 90 percent of licensed marriages in 1841 were conducted by the Church of England. Even in Wales, where nonconformism was widespread, the corresponding figure was 88 percent. Long-run trends in industrialization, urbanization, and religious affiliation nonetheless favored the Liberals. These trends gradually made constituencies less agricultural, less Anglican, and less aristocratic, such that over time the set of constituencies in which both Conservatives and Liberals could reasonably expect to win increased.

These long-run changes were catalysts of electoral contestation, but they did not operate in isolation. Modernization theorists have long emphasized the role that literacy plays in fostering democracy (e.g., Coppedge 1997; Lerner 1958; Lipset 1959; Simpson 1997; Vanhanen 2004), and many scholars have similar arguments with respect to Britain's political development (Cox 1987, 120–121; Hanham 1959, 109–113; Stokes et al. 2013; Vincent 1966). We agree that the spread of literacy and cheap newspapers encouraged electoral contestation by significantly lowering the transaction costs of fighting elections.

In our view, however, the advantages of literacy, cheap print, and abundant news media accrued disproportionately to nonincumbent challengers. This was so for two reasons. First, in an environment where political communication was heavily reliant on face-to-face interaction, incumbents with long-standing reputations and intimate contacts in a constituency enjoyed an advantage over relatively unknown challengers. The spread of literacy and the rise the penny press allowed challengers to communicate their campaign messages and mobilize their supporters more effectively, particularly as the electorate grew in size. Second, the complexity of the voter registration system that was put in place by the First Reform Act left illiterate voters ill-equipped to defend their franchise in the registration courts (Thomas 1950). The system tended to perpetuate an incumbency advantage because the better-organized side – usually the incumbent's – could systematically challenge opponents' voting qualifications and remove them from the electoral register. Illiterate voters were vulnerable to such

---

[1] This does not imply that the Conservatives won or ought to have won every general election. In fact, the Conservatives spent much of this period in opposition. The proposition is, rather, that the Conservatives would have been defeated even more frequently and more thoroughly had the underlying basis of the party system not been so strongly in their favor.

tactics, but the spread of literacy among the electorate reduced their effectiveness. In this way, the spread of literacy improved challengers' prospects and encouraged them to contest elections.

Once contested elections became established and frequent events, the cost of fighting elections via bribery, treating, and patronage increased. The further extension of the franchise in 1867 and 1884 and the natural growth of the electorate over time simultaneously amplified these cost pressures and weakened the marginal effect of candidates' expenditures on electoral outcomes. In multimember constituencies, copartisan candidates could offset these economic pressures by forming party slates that allowed them to split the overhead costs of an election campaign. A key stumbling block to the formation of party slates was what we label the *financial free-rider problem*. In double-member constituencies, where each elector had two votes, a voter could either cast one vote apiece to two candidates or "plump" (i.e., cast a single vote) for one candidate. Voters who cast two votes could also choose to give their votes to candidates of the same party or to split them between candidates of different parties. The open voting system that operated up to 1872 meant that party ballots could not be used to coordinate the manner in which electors voted. Consequently, there was an inherent risk that a candidate would make a significant financial contribution to a joint campaign only to find that his contribution worked to get his running mate, not himself, elected.

Cox (1987) argued that the decline in split voting over the course of the nineteenth century was indicative of the growth of a party-oriented electorate that was receptive to the programmatic appeals of mass parties. We are agnostic as to whether the decline in split voting was indicative of an electorate that was increasingly amenable to programmatic appeals, or simply an electorate that was increasingly animated by partisanship. Regardless of its underlying nature, we argue that it was an increasingly party-oriented electorate that ultimately resolved the financial free-rider problem: if party-oriented voters voted for the party and not for the individual candidate, then a candidate could be assured that votes would, in fact, not just flow to his running mate but to him as well.

Our work offers a theoretical account of how structural changes in the English economy and society spurred the development and evolution of the party-as-organization. Our focus thus differs from Cox's (1987); where Cox details the endogenous relationship between the party-in-the-legislature and the party-in-the-electorate, we concentrate on the evolution of the party-as-organization. This focus aligns our work with that of Stokes et al. (2013) and Camp et al. (2014), who share our interest in the changing organizational structure of local parties. However, whereas those authors focus on the declining efficacy of vote brokers as an explanation for the *demise of clientelistic competition*, we focus on candidates' willingness to run as slates as an explanation for the *emergence of partisan competition*. Finally, our study of the formation of party slates in the 1850s sets the stage for Kuo's (2018) work on the construction and programmatic efforts of Conservative and Liberal central party organizations later in the century.

1.2 Outline

Section 2 examines the onset of electoral contestation. The section develops a model which relates the onset of competition to the overhead costs of contesting a parliamentary election conditional on the probability of the candidate winning the election in the constituency: as a candidate's probability of victory increased and overhead costs declined, competition emerged. The section then undertakes an empirical examination of this model. There are two dimensions to these empirical efforts. The first involves using original data to construct a measure of the *structural bias* of the party system in a given constituency over time. Using this measure, we show that the typical constituency became less agricultural, less Anglican, and less aristocratic over time, and that these changes encouraged Liberal candidates to contest constituencies that were previously Conservative strongholds.

The second dimension of our empirical efforts relates to the impact of literacy and newspapers on electoral contestation. We use the removal of government duties on newspapers in 1855 to identify the impact of newspapers on contestation. We find that the density of newspaper consumption and the number of newspaper titles in a constituency were indicators of electoral contestation. This result is consistent with the argument that literacy and print technology encouraged electoral contestation by lowering the transaction costs of contesting elections.

Section 2 ends by examining the relationship between voter registration, literacy, and the incumbency advantage. Consistent with our argument that the complexity of the voter registration system left illiterate voters ill-equipped to protect their voting rights, we find that franchise was more extensive relative to the population in constituencies where literacy was high. We also find a robust negative relationship between an incumbent's vote shares and the literacy rate in the constituency. This is consistent with our argument that an important effect of literacy was to level the playing field between incumbents and challengers.

Section 3 sets out the economic context of mid-Victorian election campaigns. We use an original data set of the amounts that candidates spent campaigning to assess (1) the average and marginal costs of fighting an election; and (2) the marginal effects of campaign spending on election outcomes. Our analysis shows that the average cost of elections rose sharply from the 1865 election onward. At the same time, the marginal impact of campaign spending on election outcomes declined. These trends predated the expansion of the franchise in 1867, and hence we argue that it was the resumption of electoral competition along two-party lines in 1865 that was responsible for these changes. The partisan nature of the 1865 election spurred electoral contestation, and it encouraged Liberal candidates to enter and contest larger county constituencies that had been Conservative strongholds. The expansion of the franchise amplified and solidified these trends.

Section 4 deals with the emergence of party slates, or coalitions, as they were called by contemporaries. Traditionally, candidates – even those of the same party – stood independently in multimember districts (Cox 1987, 102 n. 4). By the 1860s, however, candidates of the same party tended to contest multimember districts as slates. Copartisans had strong economic incentives to form a slate and split the overhead costs of the campaign, especially as the cost of elections increased. Even so, copartisans faced a financial free-rider problem: each candidate worried that his financial contribution would ultimately work to elect his running mate and not himself. We demonstrate the existence of this collective action problem with qualitative data on the contingent contracts that copartisans entered into in an effort to limit their liabilities in any joint campaign. We then show that the financial free-rider problem faded as the British electorate became more party-oriented and began to vote on the basis of party labels. Specifically, we find that slates were more likely to emerge in constituencies where the split-voting rate was low. The financial and electoral advantage that allied candidates enjoyed meant that running independently was suboptimal. These slates were the precursors of the nationally organized parties that would structure elections from the late nineteenth century onward.

Section 5 offers a concluding discussion. Three contributions stand out to us. First, by using fine-grained and original data on literacy, we are able to demonstrate the mechanisms by which literacy and print media fostered electoral contestation. This represents an important contribution to a modernization literature that has for the most part relied on cross-national correlations to show the relevance of literacy to political development. Second, the nature of our data on candidates' campaign expenditures allows us to demonstrate that much of the increase in the unit cost of votes from 1865 onward was due to the increased frequency of contested elections. This is an important contribution because conclusions about how the extension of the suffrage altered the economics of electioneering are often made taking electoral contestation as a given. Third, our results related to the emergence and consolidation of party slates show that partisan coordination at the constituency level predated efforts by both the Liberals and the Conservatives to construct central party organizations in the 1870s. This suggests that the nationalization of electoral politics and the construction of central party organizations rested on an organic process of the sort that both Ostrogorski (1902) and Vincent (1966) emphasized. We close by comparing and contrasting the electoral politics of Victorian England with those of modern-day India. The comparison with India is intended not only to show the current relevance of political and economic history but also to place limits on our argument.

2 The Onset of Electoral Contestation

This section considers one of the Element's central questions: what made candidates increasingly willing to contest parliamentary elections, especially in constituencies that had hitherto been uncompetitive? The question is an important one for normative and theoretical reasons. From a normative perspective, electoral competition is a fundamental aspect of political contestation and therefore of democracy itself (Dahl 1973). In as much as electoral competition offers voters viable alternatives to incumbent office holders, it is also integral to electoral accountability (Przeworski et al. 1999). From a theoretical perspective, the onset of electoral competition marks an important step in the political development of a society (Caramani 2003).

We argue that electoral contestation was due to two factors: (1) the evolution of the country's socioeconomic structure, and (2) the spread of literacy and newspapers. Our argument begins with a model of electoral competition in which candidates only contest constituencies that offer them a reasonable chance of winning relative to the overhead cost of mounting a campaign. Following the logic of our model, we show that electoral contestation emerged as strongly agricultural and Anglican constituencies in which Liberal candidates faced likely defeat disappeared from England's electoral landscape. Electoral contestation was not solely a function of slow-moving socioeconomic changes, however. The spread of literacy and newspapers allowed candidates to more effectively communicate with and coordinate a larger electorate. These developments lowered the overhead cost of contesting elections and allowed challengers to fight incumbents on a more even footing.

Our focus on the relationship between literacy and newspapers and the onset of electoral contestation links our work to long-standing arguments in both history and social science about the impact of these variables on the emergence of mass democracy (Coppedge 1997; Cox 1987; Lerner 1958; Lipset 1959; Putnam et al. 1994; Simpson 1997; Stokes et al. 2013; Tocqueville 2000;

Vanhanen 2004; Vincent 1966). Many modernization theorists have observed that literacy and democratization travel together. Using original data on literacy rates in parliamentary constituencies, we show that constituencies with highly literate populations were far more likely to be contested than those with significant rates of illiteracy, and this is true across both space and time.

The modernization literature suggests two paths by which literacy fosters democratization. One is that literacy facilitates democratization mainly by altering the individual's values and perceptions (Lerner 1958; Lipset 1959; Simpson 1997). The other is that literacy and media facilitate the coordination and mobilization of large numbers of people for political action. Tocqueville (2000, 493) was an early proponent of this thesis, arguing that newspapers were the central means by which citizens in a diverse society could share ideas, coordinate their actions, and engage in associational life (see also Rueschemeyer et al. 1992; Putnam et al. 1994; Caramani 2004).

While our data do not allow us to disentangle these possibilities, we are able to show that electoral contestation increased immediately after the removal of the stamp duty on newspapers in 1855, and that it did so in relation to the consumption of newspapers and the diversity of newspaper titles in a constituency. Furthermore, we show that this effect is independent of other correlates of industrialization, such as the quantity of railway track in the constituency. This corroborates the view that literacy and print media alter politics independently of other aspects of modernization. Finally, we show a robust negative relationship between literacy and incumbency advantage. This evidence is consistent with arguments that the spread of literacy and newspapers made it easier to organize political opposition and made that opposition more effective.

The section follows in five parts. Part 2.1 provides information on electoral contestation over space and time. This part shows that the proportion of uncontested seats declined with the passage of each Reform Act, but also that there was a persistent geographical gradient to electoral contestation. Part 2.2 presents a model of electoral competition. Part 2.3 develops the measures we use in our empirical analysis, notably an index of the structural bias of the party system based on constituency-level data on agriculture, religion, and aristocratic dominance, and constituency-level measures of illiteracy rates and newspaper circulation. Part 2.4 shows that our structural bias index shifted over time in a manner that increased electoral contestation, and further that literacy was strongly related to electoral contestation independent of both the structural bias of the party system and other aspects of modernization. Part 2.5 presents evidence of the mechanisms by which literacy facilitated electoral contestation.

2.1 The Spread of Electoral Contestation

Figure 2.1 shows the percentage of contested constituencies at each general election held between 1820 and 1906; it conveys the force and scale of the disincentives to entry at the start of the period and how they weakened over time. In the two elections just prior to the First Reform Act 1832, less than 35 percent of constituencies were contested. The low level of contestation in the pre-Reform era was due to two factors. First, contested elections were incredibly expensive, and this made all candidates wary of fighting a contested election. Second, there remained vestiges of a political culture that saw parties as instruments of faction and competitive elections as disruptive (Kishlansky 1986; Manin 1997). Especially in the early part of the period and in more rural areas, electorates remained enmeshed in a web of traditional, hierarchical deference relationships (Moore 1976), and used uncontested elections as opportunities to acknowledge customary patron–client bonds and celebrate community solidarity.

The percentage of contested constituencies surged by 20 points at the 1832 election, another 20 points at the 1868 election, and 15 additional point at the 1885 election. The proximate cause of these increases was the extension of the franchise and the redistribution of seats and constituency boundaries that accompanied the First, Second, and Third Reform Acts, respectively (Lloyd 1965; Seymour 1915). Nonetheless, there was significant variation around this long-run trend, with the percentage of contested constituencies dropping below 50 percent at the 1847, 1857, and 1859 elections and below 70 percent in 1886 and 1900.

Contestation was also marked by a high degree of spatial variation. There were two dimensions to this spatial variation. First, boroughs were always more frequently contested than counties. This was a function of both the persistence of aristocratic power in rural areas and the higher cost of county elections. Second, even among the counties, there was an ostensible connection between urbanization and industrialization on the one hand, and electoral competition on the other. Figure 2.2 shows a cartogram of electoral contestation. The cartogram depicts the proportion of the twelve general elections held between 1832 and 1880 inclusive that were contested in each constituency in England and Wales. Two-thirds or more of parliamentary elections in the southeastern counties in the vicinity of London were contested, for example – a significantly higher proportion than for counties farther from the metropolis. Similarly, a vein of electoral competition extended northward along the rapidly industrializing spine of the country. Parliamentary elections in the counties of this region (e.g., Derbyshire, Warwickshire, and Staffordshire) were more likely to be

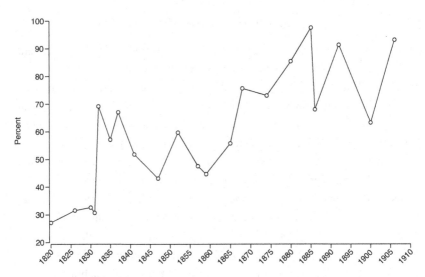

Figure 2.1 The percentage of contested constituencies at general elections in England and Wales, 1820–1906.

Sources: Craig 1977; Lloyd 1965; Philbin 1965.

contested than in the counties in more agricultural areas (e.g., Dorset, Wiltshire, and Hertfordshire).

2.2 A Model of Electoral Competition

We use a model of electoral competition to help us explain the variation in electoral contestation. The model is based on three assumptions:

1. Elections are costly to contest.
2. Constituencies are defined by structural characteristics that tend to favor candidates of one party over candidates of the other party. Agricultural and Anglican constituencies, for example, tended to favor Conservative candidates over Liberals. In contrast, Liberal candidates generally outperformed Conservatives in industrial and nonconformist constituencies. We refer to this property as the constituency's *structural bias*.
3. Candidates want to maximize the expected value of winning a parliamentary seat (i.e., the value they place on a parliamentary seat times their probability of winning it) while minimizing the costs associated with doing so. It follows that candidates will only contest a constituency for which their expected benefits exceed their associated costs.

Figure 2.3 illustrates how these assumptions combine to identify the set of constituencies that candidates are willing to contest. The x-axis arrays

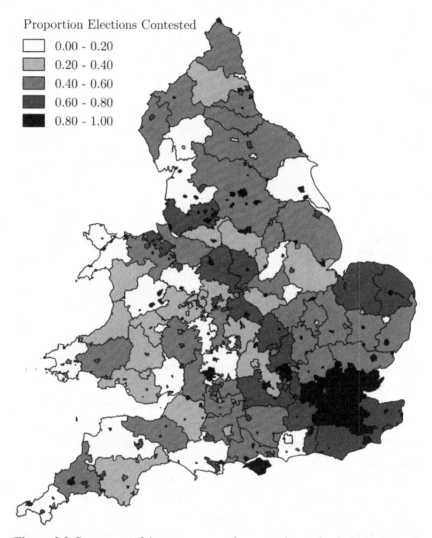

Figure 2.2 Cartogram of the percentage of contested constituencies at general elections in England and Wales, 1832–1980.

Sources: Craig 1977; Lloyd 1965; Philbin 1965.

constituencies according to their structural bias, ranging from Liberal strongholds on the left, to Conservative strongholds on the right. The upward-sloping gray curve labeled $p_C S$ represents the expected benefits to a Conservative candidate of contesting a seat as a function of the constituency's structural bias, with pC representing a Conservative candidate's subjective probability of winning the seat, and S representing the value of a parliamentary seat. The downward-sloping black curve, labeled qLS, represents the same quantity for

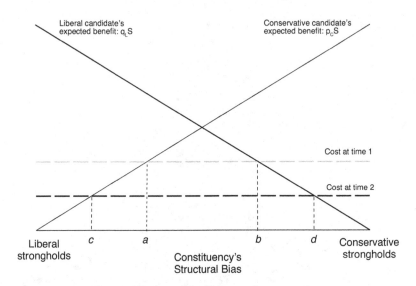

Liberal candidate's
expected benefit: $q_L S$

Conservative candidate's
expected benefit: $p_c S$

Cost at time 1

Cost at time 2

Liberal
strongholds

c   a   b   d

Constituency's
Structural Bias

Conservative
strongholds

Figure 2.3 A model of electoral contestation.

a Liberal candidate.[2] Thus, as one moves rightward along the x-axis, from constituencies that favor Liberals to those that favor Conservatives, the expected benefit of contesting the constituency decreases for the Liberal candidate and increases for the Conservative candidate.

The dashed gray line denotes the cost of contesting the election at time 1. For simplicity, we depict this cost as constant across constituencies and candidates, but we stress that this need not be the case empirically. If candidates only contest constituencies for which the expected benefits exceed the associated costs, the Conservative candidate will only contest constituencies that fall to right of *a* on the structural bias gradient, and the Liberal candidate will only contest constituencies that fall to the left of *b*. The set of contested constituencies thus falls between *a* and *b*. These are constituencies in which candidates of either party stand a reasonable chance of winning a seat, given the cost of mounting an election campaign.

The model identifies three mechanisms by which electoral contestation can spread. First, the distribution of structural bias across constituencies could shift over time such that the bulk of constituencies falls between *a* and *b* rather than, for example, to the right of *b* or to the left of *c*. We argue that the decline in

---

[2] Logic dictates that when a single-member constituency is contested by just two candidates qL = (1 − pC). However, when three or more candidates contest a multimember constituency, this need not be the case. Moreover, we approach pC and qL as subjective probabilities, and hence we do not rule out the possibility that both candidates overestimate their probability of winning the seat such that qL + pC > 1. Finally, we assume that all candidates place an equal value on a parliamentary seat, but we note that this may not be the case empirically.

agriculture, Anglicanism, and aristocratic dominance effected this sort of change. Second, the costs of contesting an election can decline. For example, if costs decline to the level depicted by the dashed black line at time 2, the set of contested constituencies will expand to include all those to the right of c and to the left of d. We argue that one effect of the spread of literacy and newspapers was to reduce the cost of electioneering and thereby to increase electoral contestation. Third, the expected value of a parliamentary seat could increase, because of an increase in either the subjective probability that candidates attached to winning the election (i.e., pC and qL) or the value that they attached to a parliamentary seat (i.e., S). This would increase the slope of the candidates' expected benefit curves and expand the set of constituencies that they would be willing to contest. We assume that the value that candidates attached to a parliamentary seat held steady over time, but we argue that another effect of the increase in literacy and the spread of newspapers was to increase the probability of nonincumbent candidates winning elections.[3]

2.3 Changes in the Structural Basis of the Party System

Changes in the socioeconomic fabric of the country opened many constituencies to electoral contestation by altering the distribution of structural bias across constituencies. As we related in our Introduction, the Conservative party was the party of agriculture, Anglicanism, and aristocratic privilege. All three of these bases of Conservative support weakened over time. Occupational data from the decennial censuses show that the percentage of the adult workforce engaged in agriculture declined from 18 percent in 1851 to 10 percent in 1911. The political influence of the landed proprietors shrank alongside the decline in agriculture, and was further disrupted by the redistribution of constituency boundaries in 1868 and 1885. By 1890, Hanham (1959, 405) estimated that proprietorial influence operated in just 11 constituencies, down from 52 in the 1840s (Gash 1953, 438–439). Finally, on the basis of data that we collected from the *Annual Report of the Registrar-General of Births, Deaths, and Marriages* (AR-BDM) we know that the proportion of marriages solemnized by the Church of England declined from 93 percent in 1841 to 64 percent in 1881.

---

[3] On one hand, the pecuniary rents that flowed from a parliamentary seat had certainly declined over time. The "Old Corruption" of the eighteenth century – that is, the widespread system of pensions, sinecures, patronage, and emolients distributed by the Crown – had largely died out by the 1850s. The House had also reorganized itself so that MPs could not directly use their positions for self-dealing (Cox 1987; Kuo 2018). On the other hand, plenty of lucrative government appointments and contracts remained in circulation (Rubinstein 1983). The increasing density of connections between industry, business, and Parliament (Kuo 2018) over the course of the nineteenth century also enhanced the economic value that British firms derived from political connections (Braggion and Moore 2013).

The net effect of these changes, on our argument, was to dilute the more staunchly Conservative constituencies to the point that Liberal candidates did not shrink from contesting them. Put in terms of the model in Figure 2.3, constituencies to the right of *d* disappeared from the electoral map and contestation increased as a result. A simple comparison of average trends in agriculture, Anglicanism, and aristocratic influence over time, on the one hand, and electoral contestation over time, on the other, does not yield a compelling test of this aspect of our model. The correlation between these two sets of factors can only be negative for the simple reason that the former all decline over time whilst the latter generally increases over time (see Figure 2.1). Our model generates an additional observable implication, however – namely, at any given election, contested elections should be concentrated in constituencies where the structural bias is moderate and candidates of both parties have a reasonable chance at winning, and uncontested elections should be concentrated in constituencies with high or low values of structural bias where only one party's candidates have a realistic chance of winning.

2.4 Literacy, the Press, and Electoral Contestation

The spread of literacy and cheap newspapers played critical roles in lowering the transaction costs of electioneering and encouraging contestation. Campaigns were heavily reliant on print media well before 1832, using broadsheets, pamphlets, and posters to inform and mobilize voters (Stokes et al. 2013). However, two aspects of the relationship between literacy, the press, and electoral politics changed after the 1832 Reform Act. The first was the adoption of a voter registration system that relied heavily on literacy for its smooth operation (Seymour 1915; Thomas 1950). The second was a sharp decline in the cost of newspapers, mainly as result of the removal of various duties and taxes beginning in 1855. As we argue, literacy and cheap and abundant newspapers were central to the onset of electoral constestation because the advantages inherent in these technologies accrued disproportionately to nonincumbent challengers.

2.4.1 Voter Registration

The voter registration system that was established in 1832 placed a premium on the electorate's literacy in as much as the onus was on the voter to claim and defend his right to vote. In the counties, the parish overseers would circulate a notice calling on qualified individuals to claim their franchise. If the individual failed to respond to this notice, his name would be left off the voters list. Borough voters were not required to exercise the same initiative as county voters, but once the overseers made public the preliminary voters lists, any elector could object to any name on the list by giving notice to the prospective voter and the overseer. A revision court would sit annually, and objectors and claimants would receive summons to press their objections and defend their voting qualifications, respectively. Even clerical errors, such as misspellings of the voter's name or address, were grounds to be struck off the electoral register (Seymour 1915, 115; Thomas 1950).

The system advantaged the literate, who could read the notices the overseers circulated, spot errors in their personal data in official documents, and read and understand any summons they received from the revising barristers. In many constituencies, party activists established registration societies to help their voters navigate the registration system, but such efforts were heavily dependent on the financial support of the incumbent MP (Gash 1983). The system thus tended to perpetuate an incumbency advantage because the better organized side – usually the incumbent's – could use the system of objections to shape the electoral register to its advantage, with illiterate voters the most vulnerable to such tactics.

This voter registration system facilitated the negotiation of uncontested elections because candidates understood that their electoral prospects hinged on their capacity to register their supporters and to object to the registration of their opponent's supporters (Salmon 2002, 20–22). The highly partisan character of the electorate (Phillips 1992; Phillips and Wetherell 1995) meant that it was often sufficient to establish an advantage on the electoral register; once this was done, the weaker party – typically the challenger's – tended to avoid a contest as it offered them only a slight chance of victory at a great expense (Gash 1953, 239–269). The rise of an electorate of literate voters, who themselves possessed the capacity to claim and defend their franchise, was thus crucial to the rise of electoral contestation because it evened the registration battle between incumbents and challengers.

2.4.2 Decline in the Cost of Printed Material

The cost of printed matter dropped sharply after 1832, partly as a result of technological improvements in printing technology and transportation (Lee 1976; Musson 1958; Weedon 2003), but mainly because of the removal of government duties on paper and advertising. Following the Peterloo Massacre of 1819, the Liverpool government had introduced the Newspaper Stamp Duties Act, one of the "Six Acts" meant to maintain social order and prevent sedition. The Act placed a duty of 4 pence on most newspapers, magazines, and pamphlets, and layered this duty on top of existing taxes and duties on paper and advertising.[4] Although many radical publishers disregarded the Stamp Act, the

---

[4] This was not a trivial sum; it would represent approximately £13 in terms of 2020 average earnings.

heavy duties on printing, advertising, and circulation stunted the growth of a mass media, especially outside of London.

The stamp duty was reduced to 1 pence in 1836, and abolished in 1855. The duties on paper were removed six years later. As these taxes and duties declined, hundreds of cheap, popular, and partisan newspapers emerged. The development of this "penny press" was facilitated by the improvement and extension of the railway and the telegraph, which helped to create a national media market. The reduction in the cost of printed material and the expansion of newspapers provided all candidates with significant economies of scale. Candidates were no longer limited to interacting with voters on a person-by-person basis, and could use newspapers and circulars to communicate with and mobilize many voters at once. The decline in the cost of print and newspapers thus reduced both the monetary and the transaction costs of electioneering and, according to our model, this should have encouraged electoral competition.

In our view, however, the advantages of cheap print and abundant news media accrued disproportionately to nonincumbent challengers. Incumbents were already recognized within and well-connected to social and professional networks in their constituencies. It was challengers who benefited most from being able to communicate directly with voters without the assistance of local intermediaries, and from being able to appeal to voters on the basis of party affiliation rather than personal ties or traditional connections. In short, the reduced cost and increased extent of print media improved the electoral prospects of nonincumbents, and this should have spurred electoral contestation.

Our arguments about the impact of literacy and newspapers on electoral contestation are more subtle than is the case in some assessments of modernization theory, where literacy (or related proxies, such as media density or education) is approached as merely one of several indicators of industrialization (e.g., Teorell 2010). Furthermore, our argument yields an observable implication that is not generated by the standard argument that newspapers lent an economy of scale to candidates' campaign efforts – that is, that the nature of the voter registration system meant that literacy encouraged contestation because it eroded the electoral advantages that incumbents enjoyed.

2.5 Data, Measures and Methods

2.5.1 Contestation

We count an election as contested if the number of candidates exceeds the number of available seats (i.e., the district magnitude). We ignore the partisan affiliation of the candidates, a decision that can be justified on two grounds. First, because candidates independently adopted and defined the ideological scope of their party affiliation, it is incorrect to assume that a contest between three Liberals, for example, offered voters no ideological choice. Voters could secure representation and accountability at such elections.[5] Second, candidates' party affiliations are not always known with certainty, and many candidates adopted ambiguous labels (e.g., independent Liberal or Liberal-Conservative). Defining contestation on the basis of party affiliation would invariably generate bias and error as we attempted to reconcile conflicting sources or differentiate between idiosyncratic labels.

2.5.2 Structural Bias

We measure the structural bias of the constituency as an additive index of three quantities: the proportion of the constituency's workforce engaged in agriculture, the proportion of marriages in the constituency solemnized by the Church of England, and the partisan affiliation of the dominant proprietorial interest, if any, in the constituency.

We rely on the decennial census for data on the proportion of the constituency's workforce engaged in agriculture. The AR-BDM provides data on the proportion of marriages in a civil registration constituency (CRD) solemnized by the Church of England in a given year. We link CRDs to parliamentary constituencies and use this statistic as a measure of the prevalence of Anglicanism in a given constituency. Finally, we code the presence of any dominant landed proprietor on the basis of information provided in Gash (1953) and Hanham (1959). We weight this variable by the proportion of the constituency's seats that the proprietor controlled (e.g.,0.5 for one seat of a double-member constituency and 1 for both seats) and give positive scores to Conservative proprietors and negative scores to Liberals proprietors. The absence of a dominant proprietor is coded as 0. We normalize each of the three components before adding them together, and then we normalize their sum so that the resulting index ranges between 0 and 1.

We denote this index as BIAS and emphasize that we take BIAS to be a function of structural factors that are themselves exogenous to electoral outcomes. We find it difficult to conceive, for example, how an election being contested or the amount that a given candidate spent at an election could materially alter the proportion of the constituency's work force engaged in agriculture or the proportion of couples in the constituency who decided to marry under the auspices of the Church of England. In addition, the families that Gash and Hanham identified as maintaining a proprietorial interest in

---

[5] One-party contests comprised 6.5 percent of contested elections held between 1832 and 1886.

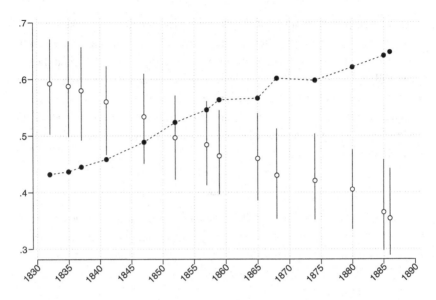

○   BIAS index

--●-- Predicted proportion of seats won by Liberals at median BIAS of each election

Figure 2.4 The interquartile range of the structural bias index (BIAS) and the predicted proportion of seats won by Liberal candidates at median levels of BIAS, 1832–1886.

a constituency had often exercised political influence in the area for decades before the 1832 Reform Act.

Figure 2.4 plots the interquartile range of BIAS at each general election held between 1832 and 1886. The structural bias of the median constituency declines steadily over time, from a high of 0.58 in 1832 to a low of 0.38 in 1886, but one can discern a pair of discrete 3-point drops in the index between 1865 and 1868 and between 1880 and 1885. The decline in both cases is due to the redistribution of constituency boundaries that accompanied the Second and Third Reform Acts, respectively. (We know that this decline was unrelated to the extension of the franchise because the three components that comprise the index are independent of the size of a constituency's electorate.) The redistribution of 1867 disenfranchised a number of proprietary boroughs, while the more wideranging redistribution of 1885 created a large number of constituencies that combined substantial rural and urban elements. In each case, the effect was to disrupt existing patterns of aristocratic dominance and to ensure that the median constituency was of more urban character after the redistribution than before.

The BIAS index is highly predictive of the relative electoral fortunes of Liberal and Conservative candidates. If we regress the proportion of seats won by Liberal candidates in a given constituency (which is observed even when an election is uncontested) on BIAS, we obtain:

$$ProportionSeatsWonbyLiberals_{jt} = \underset{(0.02)}{1.01^\dagger} - \underset{(0.04)}{0.97^\dagger BIAS_{jt}} \tag{2.1}$$

$N = 4,413$ $R^2 = 0.09$ $F(2, 4,411) = 528.4$

Robust standard errors in parentheses. $*p < 0.10$ $**p < 0.05$ $\dagger p < 0.01$

Thus, when BIAS=0, Liberal candidates are predicted to sweep the constituency's seats, and when BIAS=1, they are predicted to win none of them.

We superimpose the predicted values of this regression at the median value of BIAS at each election on Figure 2.4. In 1832, for example, Liberal candidates are predicted to win just 45 percent of the median constituency's seats; by 1886, however, they are predicted to win 65 percent. Initial conditions thus advantaged the Conservatives, but long-run trends favored the Liberals. We caution that one cannot assume that contestation is maximized, either at any general election or in a specific constituency, when BIAS=0.5. This is because Figure 2.4 provides no sense of how BIAS combines with other variables to increase or decrease contestation.

2.5.3 Illiteracy and Media Penetration

Illiteracy

We use the AR-BDM to develop a measure of the *illiteracy rate* in a given constituency at a given election. From 1839 to 1884 the AR-BDM recorded the number of grooms who *marked* the marriage register (i.e., who could not sign their names) in each civil registration constituency (CRD). Standardizing this figure by the number of marriages in the CRD and then linking CRDs to parliamentary constituencies provides us with the illiteracy rate by constituency for each election between 1832 and 1886.[6] The cross-sectional variation in illiteracy rates is greater than its variation over time, but cases in which illiteracy declines by more than 30 percent within a constituency over time are not uncommon.

Marriage registers are often used to measure literacy rates (e.g., Cipolla 1969; Mitch 1992; Stone 1969), but the technique has limitations. First, the nature of

---

[6] Until 1884, the AR-BDM reported data on grooms' signatures and the religious affiliation of marriages in a format that allows us to link CRDs to specific parliamentary constituencies. The over-time variation in these data is small enough that we are confident in using the 1884 figures for the 1885 and 1886 elections, but we are unwilling to do so for later elections. Similarly, we extend these time series backward from 1839 to 1832. Our backward projections put the average illiteracy rate at 0.38 in 1832, and this meshes well with similar estimates by other authors (see, e.g., Mitch 1992; Stone 1969).

the data presents a dilemma of overestimating literacy or underestimating illiteracy. This is because many grooms who signed their names were nonetheless functionally illiterate. The proportion of grooms who signed the register thus overestimates literacy, just as the proportion of grooms who marked the register underestimates illiteracy. Faced with this dilemma, we use the illiteracy rate in our statistical analyses because it places a minimum bound on the impact of illiteracy on electoral contestation.

A second limitation of the marriage registers is that they are unrepresentative of the general population. This is because obtaining a marriage license was expensive, and hence many poor couples married by posting bans (Stone 1969). This limitation is an advantage in this instance, however. We use the marriage registers to provide a measure of illiteracy among the electorate, not among the general male population. The electorate was defined by a property franchise, and hence it was wealthier than the general male population. It is reasonable to assume that most voters would have married via the more expensive and socially respectable means of a license and, therefore, that the marriage registers provide a representative measure of the electorate's illiteracy.

Newspaper Stamps and Titles

In addition to the illiteracy rate, we develop three measures of media presence in the constituency. Our first such measure is the total number of stamps purchased by newspapers circulating in the constituency. This provides us with a more direct measure of the newspaper circulation in a constituency than the illiteracy rate. We use the *Waterloo Directory of English Newspapers and Periodicals* to link newspaper titles to constituencies.[7] Stamp data were not reported every year, however; we have no stamp data before 1836, none for the 1847 or 1859 elections, and none after 1868. In addition, newspapers paid stamp duty after 1855 for the purpose of distributing their newspapers through the post. Thus, after 1855 the stamp data tells us more about the circulation of a newspaper outside its home territory than its presence within (where it might be sold mainly via street vendors).

Our second measure of media presence is the number of newspaper titles circulating in the constituency based on data from the British Library catalog. This may be a more pertinent measure of the media's electoral impact than the sheer number of newspaper stamps. In an era when newspapers were vociferously partisan, a diverse newspaper market, even if not large in the aggregate, was presumably indicative of a competitive electoral environment. We base this

---

[7] See www.victorianperiodicals.com/series3/index.asp. We exclude stamps purchased by trade journals (e.g., *Galvanized Iron Roofs*), advertising circulars (e.g., *Pawnbroker's Gazette*), and literary, scientific, and hobby-related magazines (e.g., *Beautiful Poetry*) from the data.

measure on a simple count of the raw number of newspaper titles that the British Library catalog assigns to the main towns in a given constituency. This measure pays no attention to differences in circulation figures across titles, and hence it counts small local papers on par with large regional newspapers. However, the nature of the British Library's records allows us to compute this measure for each general election between 1835 and 1868.

Our third measure of media presence is the effective number of newspaper titles in a constituency. We use this measure in an effort to assess media concentration in a constituency. The measure weights each newspaper title that is present in a constituency by the number of stamps purchased for that title. We compute $\frac{1}{\sum s_{ijt}^2}$ where s_{ijt} is the proportion of stamps purchased by newspaper i in constituency j in year t. For example, if newspaper A in the constituency purchased 500 stamps, and newspaper B purchased 2,000 stamps, the effective number of newspaper titles would be $1/(0.2^2 + 0.8^2) = 1.47$. This measure tells us whether the newspaper market in a given constituency was concentrated or diverse.

Figure 2.5 plots the interquartile range of the illiteracy rate across constituencies over time. The median illiteracy rate declined from 0.38 in 1832 to 0.12 in 1886. The decline is steady, albeit with larger drops in 1837, 1847, and 1859. Figure 2.5 also shows the median number of newspaper stamps per constituency on the secondary y-axis. The sharp increase in stamps at the 1857 election,

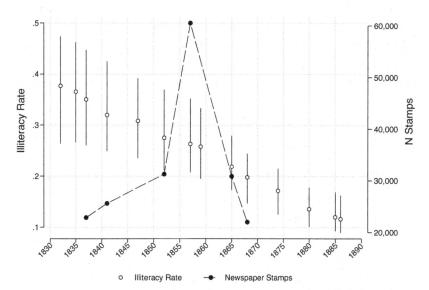

Figure 2.5 The interquartile range of constituency illiteracy rates and the median number of newspaper stamps per constituency, 1832–1886.

shortly after the removal of the stamp duty in 1855, is readily apparent. The steep drop-off in stamps after 1857 reflects the change in the usage of stamps after 1855, as discussed earlier. We do not include the median number of newspaper titles per constituency in Figure 2.5 because of its limited temporal variation: up until 1852 it was zero, and thereafter, either just two or three. Correspondingly, the median effective number of newspaper titles per constituency was just 1.25, and the average was 2. There was tremendous variation across constituencies, however: by the 1850s, London-area constituencies were home to more than 90 newspaper titles and approximately 20 effective titles.

2.5.4 Control Variables

We control for five additional variables: 1) the size of the constituency's electorate; 2) the population density of the constituency; 3) the density of railway track (i.e., km per km^2) in the constituency; 4) the district magnitude; and 5) the number of incumbents standing for re-election. The first two variables account for variation in the cost of fighting an election across constituencies. The fact that candidates had to pay to transport their supporters to the polls, and to treat them with food and drink after polling, meant that the cost of electioneering varied with the size and density of the electorate. We use the density of railway track in effort to isolate the effects of literacy from the broader effects of industrialization. The district magnitude controls for a candidate's ex ante probability of winning a seat (i.e., p and q in our model), the underlying theory being that the threshold of inclusion (i.e., the minimum vote share required to secure a seat) declines as the district magnitude increases (Lijphart 1994; Taagepera and Shugart 1989). Finally, the number of incumbents seeking re-election controls for the possibility that the electoral advantages that we have ascribed to incumbents were sufficient to deter challengers.[8]

2.5.5 Methods

Our model of electoral contestation is,

$$
\begin{aligned}
CONTEST_{jt} = {} & \beta_0 + \beta_1 ILLITERACY_{jt} + \beta_2 BIAS_{jt} + \beta_3 BIAS_{jt}^2 + \beta_4 RAILWAY_{jt} \\
& + \beta_5 M_{jt} + \beta_6 NINCUMBENTS_{jt} + \beta_7 log_2 ELECTORS_{jt} \\
& + \beta_8 DENSITY_{jt} + u_{jt}
\end{aligned}
\tag{2.2}
$$

---

[8] We cannot dismiss the possibility that the number of incumbents seeking re-election is endogenous to the probability of a contested election, but we note that the coefficients of the other variables in the models are largely unaffected by the presence or absence of the number of incumbents standing for re-election.

where CONTEST is a dummy variable equal to one when the election is contested, ILLITERACY is the illiteracy rate, BIAS is the constituency's structural bias (and $BIAS_{jt}^2$ is its square), RAILWAY is the density of railway track, M is the district magnitude, NINCUMBENTS is the number of incumbents seeking re-election, ELECTORS is the number of electors in log base 2, and DENSITY is the population density. The subscripts denote constituency j at time t. By including BIAS and $BIAS^2$ in Equation 2.2, we allow the probability of a contested election to peak in the mid-range of BIAS and decline at its extremes.

2.6 Results

We estimate four specifications of Equation 2.2 via OLS regression. The results appear in Table 2.1. The effect of illiteracy on constestation is consistently negative, regardless of whether we control for election cycle or constituency fixed effects. Thus, not only were constituencies with higher rates of illiteracy less likely to be contested than those with literate populations, it was also the case that any given constituency was more likely to be contested as its population grew more literate. The relationship between illiteracy and constestation is also robust to the presence in the model of both population density and railway density, suggesting that the relationship between illiteracy and contestation was not merely derivative of broader patterns of urbanization and industrialization.

The substantive impact of illiteracy on contestation was also a large one. Variation in the illiteracy rate across constituencies often exceeded 0.40, and many constituencies saw their illiteracy rates decrease by a similar amount between 1832 and 1886. A decline in the illiteracy rate of this magnitude is associated with an increase in the probability of a contested election of between 0.07–0.15, depending on which coefficient estimate one uses. This is, we remind readers, a lower bound estimate. By way of comparison, the average probability of a contested election over this period was 0.65.

The coefficient estimates on BIAS and $BIAS^2$ in Specifications 1–3 operate along the lines suggested by our model – that is, they indicate that contestation first increases and then decreases as BIAS ranges from 0 to 1. The probability of a contested election is thus lowest at the extremes of the BIAS index, in constituencies where structural factors strongly favored one party over the other, and highest in the mid-range of the index, in constituencies where structural factors offered candidates of both parties reasonable chances of victory. This pattern dissipates when constituency fixed effects are added to the model because the components of the BIAS index change so slowly over time that they are highly correlated with the constituency fixed effects.

Table 2.1 Regression model of contested elections, 1832–1886

	1	2	3	4
ILLITERACY$_{jt}$	−0.39†	−0.17**	−0.22†	−0.31†
	(0.07)	(0.072)	(0.082)	(0.10)
BIAS$_{jt}$	0.55**	1.09†	0.86†	−0.54*
	(0.24)	(0.23)	(0.26)	(0.30)
BIAS$_{jt}^2$	−1.08†	−1.65†	−1.24†	0.43
	(0.24)	(0.23)	(0.26)	(0.30)
log$_2$ELECTORS$_{jt}$	−0.01	−0.04†	−0.04†	0.08†
	(0.01)	(0.01)	(0.01)	(0.01)
DENSITY$_{jt}$	0.003*	0.007†	0.010†	−0.014**
	(0.002)	(0.002)	(0.002)	(0.007)
RAILWAY$_{jt}$	0.06*	0.11†	0.15†	−0.24†
	(0.03)	(0.04)	(0.04)	(0.08)
NINCUMBENTS$_{jt}$	−0.11†	−0.09†	−0.05†	−0.08†
	(0.01)	(0.01)	(0.01)	(0.01)
M$_{jt}$	0.18†	0.21†	0.12†	0.24†
	(0.02)	(0.02)	(0.02)	(0.02)
CONTEST$_{jt-1}$			0.24†	
			(0.02)	
CONSTANT	0.66†	0.74†	0.72†	−0.20
	(0.09)	(0.09)	(0.10)	(0.16)
Election fixed effects	No	Yes	Yes	No
Constituency fixed effects	No	No	No	Yes
N	4,150	4,150	3,239	4,150
R^2	0.09	0.17	0.24	0.32

Subscripts denote the election in constituency j at year t.
Cell entries are regression coefficients. Numbers in parentheses are robust standard errors.
†$p < 0.01$ **$p < 0.05$ *$p < 0.10$

We can use the coefficient estimates in Specifications 1–3 to estimate the point on the BIAS index at which contestation is maximized. Specifications 2 and 3 put this point at approximately BIAS=0.34, which is close to the mean level of BIAS at the 1885 general election. On the one hand, this is simply a curve-fitting result, with the least squares algorithm constrained to placing the maxima near the mean level of the most highly contested election in the sample. On the other hand, the fact that contestation is maximized at a point that is well off to the Liberal end of the index is indicative of how strongly the structural bias of the party system in the early decades of the century favored the

Conservatives. It is consistent also, however, with the possibility that Liberal candidates confronted systematically higher entry costs than Conservatives, and that the onset of contestation was contingent on the structural bias of the party system tilting strongly enough in the Liberals' favor to offset their higher entry costs.

The third specification of Equation 2.2 adds a lagged dependent variable ($CONTEST_{jt-1}$) to the model. The coefficient on $CONTEST_{jt-1}$ shows that a constituency having been contested at one election increases the probability of the constituency being contested at the next election by 0.24. This result shows that electoral contestation was path dependent, and that once electoral contestation took root in a constituency, it tended to persist over time.

The coefficients on $\log_2 ELECTORS_{jt}$, $DENSITY_{jt}$, and $RAILWAY_{jt}$ indicate that smaller, denser, and more industrialized constituencies were more likely to be contested than large, dispersed, nonindustrialized constituencies. The contrast is essentially between mid-sized towns, such as Coventry or Ipswich, where elections were always competitive, and the counties, where elections frequently went uncontested. We note that the coefficients on $\log_2 ELECTORS_{jt}$, $DENSITY_{jt}$, and $RAILWAY_{jt}$ all switch signs once constituency fixed effects are included in the model (see Specification 4). This indicates that within each constituency, the size of the electorate, density of the population, and industrial base tended to increase over time, as did the probability of a contested election. The cross-sectional effects in Specifications 1–3 are therefore more reliable guides to the underlying relationship between electorate size, and population and railway density, on the one hand, and electoral contestation, on the other.

All four specifications also show that the probability of a contested election increases with the district magnitude. This result runs against the historical argument that dual-member constituencies facilitated compromises to avoid contested elections (Gash 1953, 240). The results also indicate that incumbents operated as significant deterrents to contestation. Holding constant the district magnitude, each additional incumbent standing for re-election reduced the probability of a contested election by 0.05–0.11, depending on the specification. This effect is consistent with our argument that the electoral environment advantaged incumbents.

2.7 Mechanisms

2.7.1 The Impact of Newspapers

The results in Table 2.1 show a robust negative correlation between illiteracy and contestation, but they do not identify the mechanism by which illiteracy stunted contestation and by which literacy encouraged it. The most straightforward explanation of how literacy encouraged contestation is via newspapers. Newspapers lowered the cost to candidates of communicating with and organizing their supporters, thereby lowering the barriers to entering a constituency and contesting the election. On this argument, an increase in the supply of newspapers in a constituency should increase the probability of a contested election.

We test this hypothesis by using the removal of the government duties on newspapers to identify the impact of newspapers on electoral contestation. We lack the data needed to estimate the impact of the reduction in the stamp duty in 1836, and hence we confine our attention to the abolition of the stamp duty in 1855 and the removal of the newsprint duty in 1861. We know that the reduction in the price of newspapers as result of these duties being removed dramatically increased the supply of newspapers, and hence we should observe a spike in contestation shortly after these duties are removed. The elimination of these duties applied to all constituencies simultaneously, however, and hence we lack a set of constituencies that can serve as control cases. All we can do, given the structure of the data, is to estimate the difference of the impact of print media on electoral contestation before and after the removal of these duties. We do this by estimating the following equation:

$$CONTEST_{jt} = \alpha_1 PRINT_{jt} + \alpha_2 \sum \tau_t T_t + \alpha_3 PRINT \times \sum \tau_t T_t$$

$$+ \sum \lambda_k X_{jt} + \sum \delta_j D_j + u_{jt} \qquad (2.3)$$

where $PRINT_{jt}$ is a measure of the constituency's exposure to print media, $\sum \tau_t T_t$ is a vector of election fixed effects, $PRINT_{jt} \times \sum \tau_t T_t$ is a set of interactions between $PRINT_{jt}$ and the election fixed effects, X_{jt} is a vector of control variables, and $\sum \delta_j D_j$ is a set of constituency fixed effects. The vector X_{jt} contains all the variables in our initial model of electoral contestation (see Equation 2.2). The print–election interactions are the key to the model. If print media spurred electoral contestation, the coefficients on the interaction terms in the elections just after 1855 should be positive and larger in magnitude than the coefficients on the interaction terms in the elections prior to 1855.

We have four measures of the demand and supply of print media in a constituency: the illiteracy rate itself, which theoretically captures the consumption of print media; the raw number of newspaper titles in the constituency, as indicated in the British Library database; the number of stamps purchased by newspapers in the constituency; and the effective number of newspaper titles in the constituency – that is, titles weighted by stamps. The density of the London media market (which was more than ten times greater than that in the rest of the country), the close proximity of the London-area constituencies to one another, and the heavy flow of traffic between them means that we cannot accurately assign stamps and titles to individual constituencies within the metropolitan area. For this reason, we exclude the ten London boroughs from the analysis. Even with the analysis limited in this fashion, the data exhibit enormous variation in the number of stamps, ranging from zero (in small constituencies in the 1830s) to more than one million in cities such as Liverpool and Manchester. Given this huge range, we measure the number of stamps and titles in log base 2. This provides an intuitive meaning to the resulting coefficient, i.e., indicating the marginal effect of doubling the number of newspaper stamps or titles in a constituency.

The large number of interaction terms in Equation 2.3 makes it cumbersome to present the coefficient estimates in tabular form, and so we present these results graphically in Figure 2.6. Panel 1 of Figure 2.6 shows the estimated marginal effect of the constituency's illiteracy rate on the probability of the election in that year being contested. The spikes delimit the 90 percent confidence intervals of these estimates. The two vertical reference lines indicate the abolition of the newspaper stamp duty in 1855 and the removal of the duty on newsprint in 1861, respectively. The marginal effect of illiteracy on the probability of a contested election is indistinguishable from zero until 1859, whereupon it declines to –0.70. The marginal effect declines again at the 1865 election, to –1.08. Given that the illiteracy rate declined by 0.05 between 1857 and 1865, these figures suggest that the improvement in the literacy rate coincided with an increase in the probability of a contested election of up to 0.06 in this time frame.

The second panel of Figure 2.6 shows the marginal effect of the raw number of newspaper titles (in log base 2) on the probability of a contested election. These data show a steady increase on the marginal effect of newspaper titles on electoral contestation between 1837 and 1857, albeit with a sharp increase at the 1857 election just after the abolition of the stamp duty in 1855. The 1857 coefficient indicates that doubling of the number of newspaper titles in a constituency increased the probability of a contest at the 1857 general election by 0.05. The effect quickly subsides, and is statistically significant only at the 1857 election.

Panel 3 shows the marginal effect of the number of stamps that newspapers purchased (in log base 2) on the probability of a contested election. As with newspaper titles, the marginal effect of stamps on contestation spikes at the 1857 election. In contrast to the raw number of titles, however, the effect of stamps on contestation persists until 1865 (we have no stamp data for 1859), before declining in 1868. At its peak, doubling of the number of newspaper

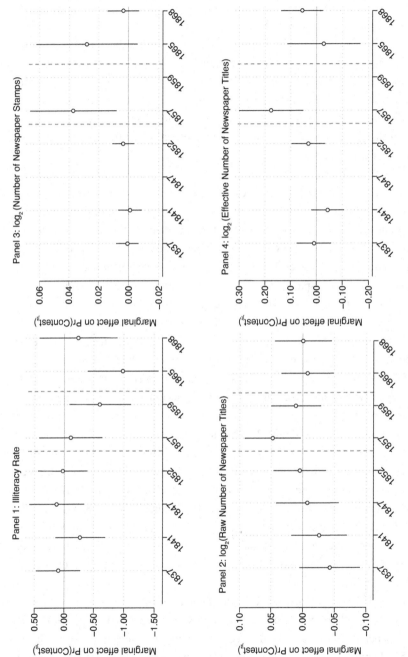

Figure 2.6 The marginal effect of literacy and newspapers on electoral contestation.

stamps in a constituency is associated with an increase in the probability of a contested election of approximately 0.04.

The fourth panel of Figure 2.6 shows the marginal effect of effective number of newspaper titles on the probability of a contested election – that is, the number of titles weighted by the number of stamps each newspaper purchased. The trend in the coefficients is similar to that in Panels 2 and 3: spiking in 1857, and then quickly declining. In a mid-sized town – take Coventry as an example – the effective number of titles increased from 1 to approximately 2 between 1852 and 1857 – that is, roughly doubling in size immediately after the stamp duty was removed. Such an increase would have coincided with an increased probability of a contested election of 0.17.

We can speculate that the decline in these effects by 1868 was due to literacy and newspaper circulation reaching a critical density or being overwhelmed by the effects of the Second Reform Act. We must also acknowledge that none of our measures is beyond reproach, and that our coefficients are based on a simple before-and-after comparison (albeit holding election and constituency fixed effects constant), not a more persuasive difference-in-difference research design. Even so, the results are consistent across all four measures of media exposure. The timing of the effects is also broadly correct, all of them increasing sharply at the 1857 or 1859 elections, shortly after the abolition of the stamp duty in 1855.

2.7.2 Literacy, Voter Registration, and the Incumbency Advantage

Our discussion in Section 2.4 linked illiteracy to contestation via the existence of an incumbency advantage. We made two arguments to this effect. The first was that the procedural nature of the registration system left illiterate voters ill-equipped to defend their franchise. This, coupled with the fact that incumbents were better placed to use the system of objections to remove opponents from the register, imparted an electoral advantage to incumbents. As illiteracy declined, voters were better able to defend their right to vote and this incumbency advantage waned. The second was that the advantages of cheap and plentiful newspapers disproportionately accrued to challengers who lacked the recognition and networks that incumbents possessed. The spread of newspapers thus evened the electoral odds between challengers and incumbents.

These arguments imply two testable hypotheses. First, if illiterate voters were less able to defend their franchise, then we should observe that the franchise is less extensive relative to the population in constituencies where the illiteracy rate is high. Second, to the extent that any incumbency advantage was contingent on the electorate's literacy, we should observe literacy interacting with incumbency, such that incumbents are strong when illiteracy is high and weak when it is low.

The Extent of the Franchise

We measure the extent of the franchise in a constituency by dividing the number of registered electors in a constituency by its population. We denote this variable FRANCHISE. We then test the hypothesis that the extent of the franchise varied inversely with the illiteracy rate by regressing FRANCHISE on the illiteracy rate (ILLITERACY) in the constituency.

Because the franchise rested on the voter's capacity to pay the taxes on a property of a certain ratable value, we require some means to control for economic conditions in the constituency. When times were good, a voter might have the income to pay the necessary taxes, and the property itself might rise above the ratable value. Conversely, when times were bad, the voter might be unable to afford to pay the necessary taxes and the property value might also fall below the statutory threshold. We use the marriage rate (MARRY) in the constituency as measure of the economic conditions in the constituency. The Malthusian assumption underpinning this variable is that the marriage rate is positively correlated to economic conditions, with couples delaying marriage and children when economic conditions are poor, and marrying and starting families when economic conditions are good. Correspondingly, we expect more individuals to be able to meet the property qualification for the franchise when the marriage rate is high. A dummy variable for boroughs (BORO) accounts for the different basis of the franchise across the borough and county constituencies. Our regression model is thus,

$$FRANCHISE_{jt} = \beta_0 + \beta_1 ILLITERACY_{jt} + \beta_2 BORO_{jt} + \beta_3 MARRY_{jt} + u_{jt}$$
$$(2.4)$$

and the expectation is that $\beta_1 < 0$.

Table 2.2 presents OLS estimates of the coefficients in Equation 2.4. There are two points to take away from Table 2.2. First, there is a robust negative relationship between the illiteracy rate and the extent of the franchise in a constituency. This negative relationship persists regardless of whether or not we control for constituency fixed effects in addition to election fixed effects (Specifications 2 and 4), and regardless of whether or not the analysis is restricted to the period before the Second Reform Act (Specifications 1 and 2) or extended to the eve of the Third Reform Act (Specifications 3 and 4). Second, the impact of illiteracy on the extent of the franchise was potentially substantial. This is because up until 1867 the franchise was limited whereas the illiteracy

Table 2.2 Illiteracy and the extension of the franchise

	1832–1880		1832–1867	
	1	2	3	4
ILLITERACY	−0.019†	−0.017**	−0.038†	−0.008*
	(0.004)	(0.008)	(0.004)	(0.004)
MARRY	0.059*	−0.095	0.157†	0.048**
	(0.033)	(0.046)	(0.026)	(0.022)
BORO	0.037†		0.020†	
	(0.001)		(0.001)	
Constituency fixed effects	No	Yes	No	Yes
Election fixed effects	Yes	Yes	Yes	Yes
R2	0.53	0.76	0.18	0.85
N	4090		3019	

Subscripts denote the election in constituency j at year t.

Cell entries are regression coefficients. Numbers in parentheses are robust standard errors.

$^{†}p < 0.01$ $^{**}p < 0.05$ $^{*}p < 0.10$

rate was high and varied widely across constituencies. Given the magnitude of the coefficients in Table 2.2, we estimate that 5–20 percent of the variation in the extent of the franchise across constituencies was due to differences in their respective illiteracy rates.[9] These results are fully consistent with our argument that the registration system left illiterate voters ill equipped to defend their voting rights.

The Interaction between Illiteracy and Incumbency

We test the hypothesis that the incumbent advantage varied with illiteracy by regressing candidates' vote shares (VOTE) on an interaction between the constituency's illiteracy rate (ILLITERACY) and a dummy variable that identifies the candidate as an incumbent or a challenger (INCUMBENT). We define an incumbent as having represented the constituency in question in the parliamentary term immediately preceding the election. Incumbency is thus defined by the representation of a specific constituency; an MP who sought re-election in a different constituency is designated as a challenger, not an incumbent. This accords with our argument that the incumbency advantage flowed from the

---

[9] These figures are underestimates because we have computed FRANCHISE on the basis of the total population of the constituency for reasons of data availability, whereas voting rights were limited to males aged 21 and over.

incumbent's influence over the constituency's electoral register and his local reputation and knowledge.

On the basis of our theoretical model, we expect Conservative candidates' vote shares to increase with the constituency's structural bias, and for Liberal candidates' vote shares to decrease with the constituency's structural bias. We also expect all candidates' vote shares to decline as the district magnitude increases. This is because the number of candidates contesting the election is theoretically one greater than the number of seats available (Cox 1997), and as more candidates enter the election, the average vote share can be expected to decline. Hence, we control for both BIAS and M in the regression below.

The district magnitude and the three components of the BIAS index are all plausibly exogenous to candidates' vote shares. (It is difficult for us, for example, to imagine a mechanism by which more people choose to get married by the Church of England because the Conservative candidate wins the election.) However, many other variables that might plausibly explain a candidate's vote share are either plainly endogenous to the candidate's vote share or unobserved. A well-liked incumbent, for example, does not need to spend a large amount of money on his re-election campaign, but we cannot directly observe his popularity and hence the relationship between the money that he does spend and his observed vote share is misleading. We grapple with this problem at length in Section 3. Our strategy here is to rely on election cycle, constituency, and candidate fixed effects to control for the effects of omitted variables.

Our regression model is:

$$
\begin{aligned}
VOTE_{ijt} = \beta_0 &+ \beta_1 INCUMBENT_{ijt} + \beta_2 ILLITERACY_{jt} + \beta_3 INCUMBENT_{ijt} \\
&\times ILLITERACY_{jt} + \beta_4 BIAS_{jt} + \beta_5 PARTY_{ijt} + \beta_6 BIAS_{jt} \\
&\times PARTY_{ijt} + \beta_7 M_{jt} + \sum \tau_t T_t + \sum \delta_j D_j
\end{aligned}
\tag{2.5}
$$

where in addition to the variables described above, PARTY is a dummy variable that distinguishes Conservatives from Liberals, $\sum \tau_t T_t$ is a vector of election cycle fixed effects, and $\sum \delta_j D_j$ is a vector of constituency fixed effects. We estimate Equation 2.5 via OLS, under the expectation that both β_1 and β_3 are greater than zero.

Figure 2.7 provides a graphical representation of our estimates. Each panel of Figure 2.7 shows the predicted vote share of a challenger and an incumbent under conditions of low illiteracy and high illiteracy controlling for a different set of fixed effects. The low illiteracy rate is 0.10, and the high illiteracy rate is 0.45, values that correspond to the 10th and 90th percentiles of illiteracy in our data.

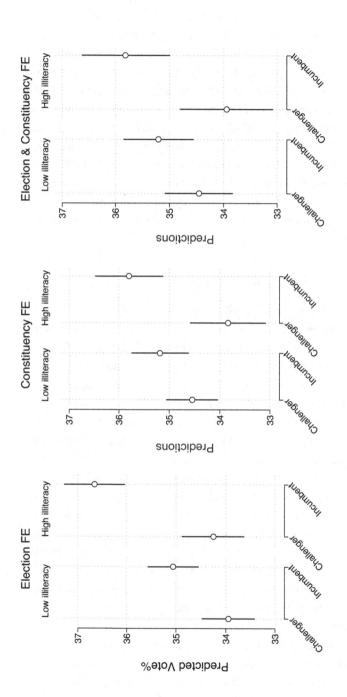

Figure 2.7 The interactive effect of incumbency and illiteracy on candidates' vote shares.

Each panel holds constant a different set of fixed effects. The first panel controls for election-specific fixed effects so that the comparison between challengers and incumbents accounts for the average vote share of candidates at the same election, albeit in different constituencies. The second panel controls for constituency-specific fixed effects, so that the comparison is between challengers and incumbents within the same constituency, albeit at different elections. The data exhibit the same pattern in both instances: incumbents' vote shares exceed challengers' vote shares by approximately 2 percent when illiteracy is high, but by less than 1 percent when literacy is low. The third panel controls for election and constituency-specific fixed effects. The results are thus based on a comparison of challengers and incumbents who are contesting the same constituency at the same election. Again, one observes that incumbents outperform challengers at the polls when illiteracy is high but not when it is low.

2.8 Conclusion

What made candidates increasingly willing to contest parliamentary elections, especially in constituencies that had hitherto been uncompetitive? The answer is that a shift over time in the socioeconomic forces that shaped the English party system generated incentives to electoral competition. The modal constituency became less agricultural, less Anglican, and less aristocratic, and, for those reasons, far more conducive to the electoral success of Liberal candidates. It is plausible, on our evidence, that Liberal candidates confronted systematically higher entry costs and that contestation took hold once the structural bias of the party system tilted strongly enough in their favor to offset their higher entry costs. Furthermore, we can infer that Conservative candidates coped with these socioeconomic changes from the fact that contestation increased rather than declined even as the structural bias of the party system grew to favor the Liberals. We can speculate that this was due in part to the Conservative leadership's effective use of the redistribution of seats and boundaries to offset the structural bias of the party system (McLean 2001). It is also likely, however, that Conservative electoral prospects were fairly robust to the decline of agriculture and Anglicanism simply because elections after 1880 increasingly revolved around the Irish Question and class politics.

The spread of literacy worked alongside these socioeconomic changes to spur electoral contestation. Contestation increased shortly after the abolition of the stamp duty on newspapers in 1855, and it did so in constituencies where the consumption of newspapers was heaviest and where the newspaper market was the most diverse. This key result corroborates the widely held thesis that the spread of newspapers, or print media more generally, allowed candidates to more efficiently communicate with and mobilize their supporters.

Some have argued that literacy does more than simply facilitate communication and mobilization; it also alters the individual's perceptions and horizons. Our evidence does not speak directly to this latter possibility, but it does show that literate voters were better able to defend their voting rights than illiterate ones. Furthermore, literacy reduced the in-built advantages that incumbents enjoyed. In leveling the playing field between incumbents and challengers, literacy encouraged electoral contestation. Moreover, because of the fine-grained nature of our data, we are able to show that the effects of literacy on electoral contestation operated independently of industrialization and urbanization, and that they operated both across constituencies and over time. This is a substantial advance relative to what we have been able to learn about the relationship between literacy and political modernization on the basis of cross-national measures and correlations.

3 The Economics of Elections

This section departs from the observation that the electoral contestation that took root in many constituencies after 1832 frequently revolved around the clientelistic exchange of private goods for votes. Competing for votes on this basis became increasingly problematic as the electorate grew in size. A large electorate presented campaigns based on the exchange of private goods for votes with two problems. First, the number of votes that a candidate could purchase for a fixed sum comprised an ever-smaller fraction of a growing electorate (Cox 1987, 57). Second, the transaction costs of distributing private goods to large numbers of voters escalated rapidly, both because each voter had to be paid and because a correspondingly large number of agents had to be hired to arrange these payments (Stokes et al. 2013, 215–216).

In contrast, programmatic appeals can be disseminated economically to a large and literate electorate via newspapers and other print media, and without the need for a dense network of paid agents (Kitschelt and Wilkinson 2007; Stokes et al. 2013). A programmatic electoral strategy thus offers candidates significant economies of scale relative to a clientelistic strategy. Eventually, the electorate grows large enough that candidates are better off abandoning clientelism and contesting elections on the basis of programmatic appeals that stress the delivery of public goods. In the British case, for example, Stokes and colleagues show that the average cost of votes (i.e., the total amount spent by all candidates at a given general election divided by total number of votes cast) declined quickly after 1885 in a manner that suggests that candidates were reliant on programmatic appeals by that time.

While we largely agree with this theoretical account of the development of programmatic politics in Britain, there are two problems with the argument as it stands. First, both Cox and Stokes et al. take electoral contestation as given. This overlooks the role that the increased frequency of contested elections played in driving up electioneering costs. Second, Cox and Stokes et al. focus on different aspects of the relationship between money and votes. Stokes et al. stress how the high transaction costs of organizing bribery in a large constituency increased the unit cost of votes. This perspective casts the *average cost of votes* as the critical variable. Cox's argument, however, highlights the "diminished electoral return" (Cox 1987, 57) to bribery in large constituencies. This line of argument places the focus on the *marginal effect of money* on electoral outcomes.

The economic basis of campaigns rests on both of these quantities, but the relationship between them is neither direct nor obvious. If programmatic strategies are perfect substitutes for clientelistic strategies, the average cost of votes and the marginal effect of money on votes may both decline: the former because programmatic campaigns are cheap; the latter because election outcomes hinge on policies, not the amounts that candidates spend. An alternative, however, is that clientelistic and programmatic strategies are complements, the exchange of private goods for votes being used to insure the candidate in the event that voters dislike their party's policies. Under this alternative, average spending may decline significantly (because competition is mostly programmatic) even while the marginal effect of money on votes remains high. The logic here is that the small spending advantage that one candidate enjoys over another may nonetheless be sufficient to deliver victory.

For these reasons, we think that it is important to use more refined data to assess the economic basis of nineteenth-century parliamentary elections. We use original data from published accounts and election petitions to estimate the average costs of elections, and to assess how these costs responded to the increases in both the size of the electorate and the frequency of electoral contestation. We also consider the marginal effect of candidates' expenditures on electoral outcomes. Our analysis identifies the 1865 elections as a turning point, with the marginal effect of money on votes dropping to almost zero even while the fixed cost of fighting a contested election rose sharply. This evidence suggests that the economic pressures on candidates to renounce clientelistic electoral tactics were mounting even before the franchise was extended in 1868. The resumption of electoral competition along clear two-party lines by 1865 appears to us as the most plausible cause of these important changes in the economic basis of mid-Victorian election campaigns.

3.1 Data Sources

Our main source of data on campaign expenditures is the published accounts of elections expenses that candidates filed with the House of Commons in accordance with the Corrupt Practices Act, 1854. These data are numerous (N=4,365) and comprehensive, and for those reasons have been widely employed (see, e.g., Coates and Dalton 1992; Kam 2017; Mares and Zhu 2015). The line items of the published accounts provide insight into the range of materials and services that campaigns purchased. There were five general categories of expenses: 1) fees charged by local officials for the conduct of the election; 2) wages of paid agents, typically a local solicitor and a number of clerks and messengers; 3) rental costs of committee rooms; 4) printing and advertising costs; and 5) the cost of conveying voters to the polls.

It is analytically useful to conceive of some of these costs as fixed (e.g., the retainer paid to a local solicitor) and others as varying with the size of a constituency's electorate. Printing costs, for example, increased with the size of the electorate. George Ade, an election agent, described the use of printed material at elections in Marylebone, which had an electorate of 20,000 by the 1850s:

> It is customary to send a circular to every individual by post; that, of course, is a large expense. Then there are various other letters sent, and then polling-cards are sent to every individual, so that the expense of printing is very considerable (P.P. 1854 [329], 206, §2623).[10]

Fixed costs tended to run between £300–500 in the boroughs and perhaps twice that in the counties. This was probably the minimum cost of mounting a campaign in a small borough, and it aligns with the amount of the subsidy that a few fortunate candidates received from the central party organizations (Gash 1983). Variable costs would fall to almost zero at uncontested elections.

The published expenditures have two drawbacks: they exist only from 1854 onward, and they systematically underestimate expenditures because candidates did not disclose sums spent on illegal activities, such as bribery (Seymour 1915, 409–410). We offset these weaknesses by employing a second source. This is an original data set of campaign expenditures as revealed by election petitions. The investigations that accompanied an election petition often revealed what candidates actually spent on elections, including sums spent on bribery, treating, and the like. These data also give us information on the cost of elections prior to 1854. That said, these "revealed" expenditures

---

[10] Denotes a citation from the House of Commons *Parliamentary Papers*, read as year, paper number (in square brackets), page, and section number.

are not numerous (N=583), and they are concentrated almost exclusively on borough elections. Given the strengths and weaknesses of the two data sources, our approach is to conduct the analyses using both the published and revealed expenditures to the extent possible. Where both data sources agree on the trend or direction of a relationship, we are more confident in the results.

3.2 Average Costs over Time

Figure 3.1 shows published expenditures at contested elections in both county and borough constituencies, and revealed expenditures (i.e., those revealed by election petitions) at contested elections in borough constituencies. The average

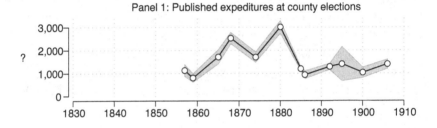

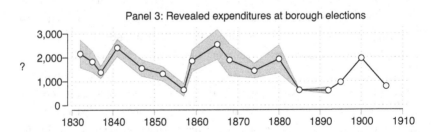

Expenditures denominated in 1906 GDP–deflated terms

Shaded areas indicate 95% confidence intervals

Figure 3.1 Candidates' average campaign expenditures at parliamentary elections, 1832–1886.

cost of a contested county election increased from £2,780 in 1857 (n=44) to £3,800 in 1880 (n=133). One assumes that much of this increase was due to the increased size of the electorate. This is because a large fraction of the expense of a county election was related to the cost of conveying votes to the polls; as the electorate expanded, these costs increased. These figures may also understate the full expense of a contested county election. If we compare the expenditures for county elections to the revealed expenditures for borough elections, we have to accept either that many borough elections were as expensive as county elections, or that some fraction of the full expenditure at county elections was routinely kept off the books.

The latter possibility is more likely. While bribery was rarely practiced at county elections, treating supporters with food and drink after voting was commonplace and expensive (P.P. 1835 [547], 93–94, §1641–1649). The ambiguous legal status of treating provided incentives for candidates at county elections to conceal expenditures related to treating. This intuition is consistent with the fact that the thirty revealed expenditures that we have for county elections place the average cost of a contested county election at £5,800. As with the boroughs, this is approximately twice the average published cost.

We are confident in this estimate because additional evidence suggests that the revealed expenditures are roughly representative of the true cost of electioneering. In particular, the average expenditure of £1,800 and minimum expenditure of £1,000 for contested borough elections provided by our revealed data accord with qualitative evidence on the cost of electioneering. Questioned by Royal Commissioners as to whether his expenditures of £1,200 to £1,400 at Totnes in 1865 did not strike him as "a very large sum to be asked for comparatively so small a borough?" John Pender replied:

> Well, I fancy it did not strike me much, because I had often been talking to members of parliament, asking the expenses of boroughs, the general, what you may call not legal expenses; still they were legalised by use and wont on the part of members of parliament, that every borough more or less had its price; and I simply looked upon Totnes as perhaps one of the least expensive, not most expensive, of boroughs that return members of parliament. (P.P. 1867 [3776], 700, §39261)

Pender noted that he had also inquired about contesting Great Grimsby and was told that that constituency would cost him £1,000 or £1,200. Such sums did not strike Pender as unusually large, "because [he] had so frequently heard larger sums named" (P.P. 1867 [3776], 700, §39265).

The revealed expenditures peak at the 1841, 1865, and 1880 general elections. (We discount the fourth peak, at the 1900 elections, because it is due to a single data point.) The common theme that binds these three elections is less one of bitter struggles over grand policies (although the Corn Laws were at the heart of the 1841 election) and more one of unmitigated electoral corruption (O'Leary 1962). The published costs corroborate the spike in electioneering expenditures in 1880 and their rapid decline from 1885 onward. The key difference between the revealed and published series centers on when costs began to increase toward the second peak. The revealed expenditures show the increase starting in 1859 and peaking in 1865. In contrast, the published figures show the increase starting in 1865 and peaking in 1868. As we argue, the former dates emphasize the role that more extensive electoral contestation played in the increase in electioneering costs, whereas the latter dates emphasize the role that the extension of the suffrage played in the increase in electioneering costs.

3.2.1 Estimating Candidates' Cost Functions

The variation in candidates' average expenditures shown in Figure 3.1 is due to a combination of changes in the price of votes over time and in the composition of the set of contested constituencies from one election to the next. A multivariate model of electioneering costs helps us to assess how these factors altered the cost of votes. We begin with a simple cost function:

$$K_{ijt} = F + c\big(V_{ijt}\big), \tag{3.1}$$

where K_{ijt} is candidate i's expenditure in constituency j at time t; F are the fixed costs of mounting a campaign; and $c(V_{ijt})$ are the variable costs, which are assumed to increase in V_{ijt}, the number of votes i receives.

We cannot estimate Equation 3.1 directly for two reasons. First, we do not observe V when the election is uncontested. Second, V is endogenous to K: candidates do not incur expenses because people vote for them; they expend funds to gain people's votes. Indeed, Victorian candidates purchased votes in direct ways that ranged from paying to transport the voter to the poll to bribing him.

Our solution to these problems is to use the BIAS index as an instrument for the number of votes a candidate wins. The idea is this: a Conservative candidate contesting a constituency with a structural bias of B and an electorate of size E should, on average, obtain EB votes, and his Liberal opponent should obtain $E(1 - B)$ votes. For example, if two Conservative candidates compete against a single Liberal in a constituency of 1,000 voters (so E=1,000) and BIAS = 0.5, we expect 500 voters to cast split votes for the two Conservatives and 500 to plump for the lone Liberal. All candidates thus receive $EB = E(1 - B) = 500$ votes. Substituting $V_{ijt} = EB_{jt}$ in Equation 3.1 for Conservative candidates, and $V_{ijt} = E\big(1 - B_{jt}\big)$ for Liberal candidates, provides a reduced-form model of candidates' costs:

$$K_{ijt} = F + c\big([EB_{jt} \times CON_{ijt}] + [E(1 - B_{jt}) \times LIB_{ijt}]\big) \tag{3.2}$$

where CON_{ijt} and LIB_{ijt} are dummy variables that identify candidate i as a Conservative or a Liberal, respectively. Thus, when CON_{ijt} and $LIB_{ijt} = 0$ and vice versa.

Because Equation 3.2 does not contain candidates' vote totals it can be estimated over both contested and uncontested elections. We capture the cost differential between contested and uncontested elections by interacting the terms on the right-hand side of Equation 3.2 with a dummy variable for contested elections ($CONTEST_{jt}$). Our regression model is then,

$$K_{ijt} = \sum \theta_t T_t \times \beta_1 \big(ELECTORS_{jt} \times BIAS_{jt} \times CON_{ijt}\big) \times CONTEST_{jt}$$
$$+ \sum \phi_t T_t \times \beta_2 \big(ELECTORS_{jt} \times (1 - BIAS_{jt}) \times LIB_{ijt}\big) \times CONTEST_{jt}$$
$$+ \sum \lambda_t T_t \times CONTEST_{jt} + \sum \gamma_k X_{jt} \times CONTEST_{jt} + \sum \tau_t T_t + u_{ijt}$$
$$\tag{3.3}$$

where $\sum \tau_t T_t$ is a set of a set of election fixed effects, and $\sum \gamma_k X_{jt}$ is a set of control variables consisting of a dummy for boroughs, the district magnitude, and constituency's population density.

Equation 3.3 reduces to $K_{ijt} = \sum \tau_t T_t$ when an election is uncontested, with the τ coefficients providing estimates of the average cost of uncontested elections at a given general election. Similarly, β_1 and β_2 provide estimates of the marginal cost of an additional (estimated) vote at a contested election to Conservative and Liberal candidates, respectively. We denominate K in hundreds of 1906 GDP-deflated pounds, and ELECTORS in hundreds of voters, so that the interpretation is that the Conservative candidate's campaign costs increase by $\beta_1 \times$ £100 for every additional 100 votes he obtains.[11]

We estimate Equation 3.3 via OLS. Figure 3.2 offers a graphical perspective on the results. For each general election of the period, Figure 3.2 shows predicted expenditures given variation in the size of the constituency's electorate and conditional on the election having been contested or uncontested. The light-shaded regions in each panel depict the 95 percent confidence intervals of these predicted expenditures, whilst the dark-shaded regions indicate the interquartile range of contested and uncontested constituency electorates, respectively. Each panel is also annotated to note the probability of a contested election in each period and the slope of the cost curve for contested elections. The latter (i.e., b) is

---

[11] We can add polynomials of candidates' estimated votes to Equation 3.3, but doing so does little to alter the substance of the results even while it complicates their interpretation.

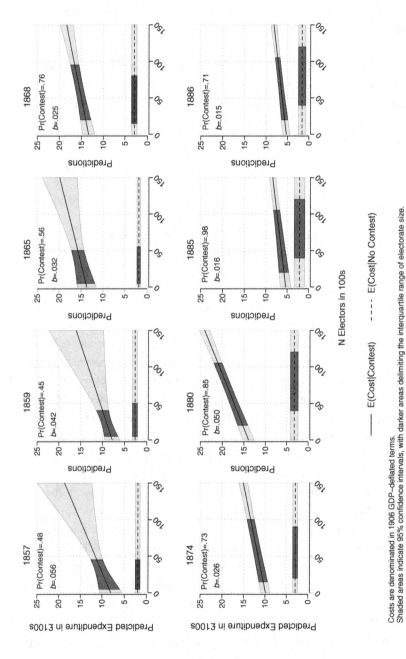

Figure 3.2 Predicted campaign expenditures at contested and uncontested elections, 1857–1886.

Costs are denominated in 1906 GDP–deflated terms.
Shaded areas indicate 95% confidence intervals, with darker areas delimiting the interquartile range of electorate size.

a weighted average of β_1 and β_2 from Equation 3.3, with weights based on the relative proportion of Conservative and Liberal candidates at that election.

If we interpret the intercept of the contested cost curve as the fixed cost of fighting a contested election, then it is clear that fixed costs increased sharply in 1865. Indeed, Figure 3.2 shows that the fixed cost of contesting an election was always large relative to the increase in costs generated by the size of the electorate. In 1865, for example, the difference between the intercepts of the cost curves for contested and uncontested elections (£1,370 and £190, respectively) puts the fixed cost of a contested election at £1,180. By comparison, a candidate's predicted expenditure in constituency of 5,000 voters, a large electorate in 1865, was £1,575. Fixed costs thus comprised 75 percent of the candidate's expenditure, and applied as much to a borough of 500 voters as to a city of 5,000. The proportion of fixed to variable costs varied from election to election but was never less than 50 percent.

The increased frequency of contested elections also drove up the amounts that candidates could expect to spend over a series of elections. Prior to 1868 an incumbent could, on average, expect the financial relief of an uncontested election at every other election, but after 1868 he could expect it only every fourth election.[12] Few parliamentary careers lasted this long. The sharp increase in the proportion of contested constituencies from 1868 onward thus represented a severe financial shock.

In theory, the transaction costs of clientelism increase rapidly as the electorate grows in size. The cost of the marginal vote at these elections should therefore increase as the electorate expands up until the point that candidates adopt programmatic electoral strategies, whereupon it should drop. The cost of the marginal vote at these elections is given by the slope of the regression lines in each panel of Figure 3.2. There is no statistical difference in these slopes across elections, albeit because the confidence bands around the 1857 and 1859 predictions are so wide. Nonetheless, if we focus on the substantive differences in the regression slopes at each election, we can discern two step-wise decreases in the marginal cost of votes: the first in 1865, and the second in 1885. Only the latter can be attributed to the extension of the franchise (via the Third Reform Act), and this clearly effected a substantial reduction in the cost of votes.

A similar analysis based on revealed expenditures shows that costs averaged £28 per 100 votes at elections before 1865, but just £8 per 100 votes at elections thereafter. The revealed expenditures also show a step-wise increase in fixed costs in 1865. This evidence points to the 1865 elections as a turning point in the

---

[12] The probability of an uncontested election was not random across constituencies, of course. Some constituencies promised the winner a series of uncontested elections, whereas others promised stiff contests at every general election.

economic basis of parliamentary election campaigns, but not one that we can easily connect to the extension of the franchise.

The Marginal Effect of Money on Votes

Cox's argument was that, all else equal, the number of votes that a fixed sum of money bought represented a smaller proportion of a large electorate than a small one. The extension of the suffrage and the natural growth of the electorate should therefore have diminished the impact of campaign expenditures on election outcomes. The data in Figure 3.3 are consistent with this argument. The panels in Figure 3.3 show scatter plots of candidates' published expenditures and their vote totals at contested elections for each general election between 1857 and 1886. Both variables are graphed in log base 2 to ease the distortion generated by outliers. We also impose lowess regression lines on the scatter plots to give a sense of the relationship between the two variables. The relationship between candidates' expenditures and their vote totals is generally positive until the passage of the Third Reform Act in 1885.

Figure 3.4 repeats this exercise using the revealed expenditures. The revealed expenditures exhibit a much less stable relationship between candidates' expenditures and their vote totals. We can identify some elections – the three elections that followed the Second Reform Act, for example – where votes increase with expenditures, but several others where there is no clear relationship between money and votes.

The smaller number of data points is one reason why the relationship between money and votes is less stable in the revealed expenditures than in the published expenditures. Another reason, however, is that the revealed expenditures disproportionately relate to highly competitive elections where high levels of spending by one side were offset by equally high levels of spending by the other.[13] These results imply a correlation between intense competition and high expenditures. In contrast, the relationship between money and votes is clearer in the published expenditures because the published expenditures do not implicitly control for the competitiveness of the election; they are drawn from a mixture of competitive elections and lop-sided elections, where one side offered only token opposition.

This raises the possibility that the impact of money on votes appears most visible at those elections where it has the least impact. A similar dynamic is observed at US Congressional elections, where the lack of a clear relationship between campaign spending and election outcomes is related to the fact that

---

[13] The revealed expenditures are more likely to be observed at elections in constituencies that fall in the mid-range of the BIAS index – that is, in constituencies where structural factors promised candidates of both parties nearly equal probabilities of victory. The margin of victory between the last-placed winning candidate and the first-placed losing candidate was also 3.6 percentage points smaller at elections where revealed expenditures are observed.

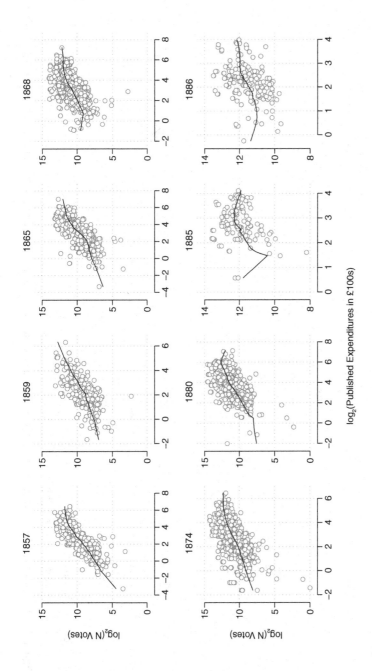

Lowess bandwidth = .5

Expenditures are denominated in 1906 GDP–deflated terms

Figure 3.3 The relationship between candidates' published campaign expenditures and their vote totals at contested elections, 1857–1886.

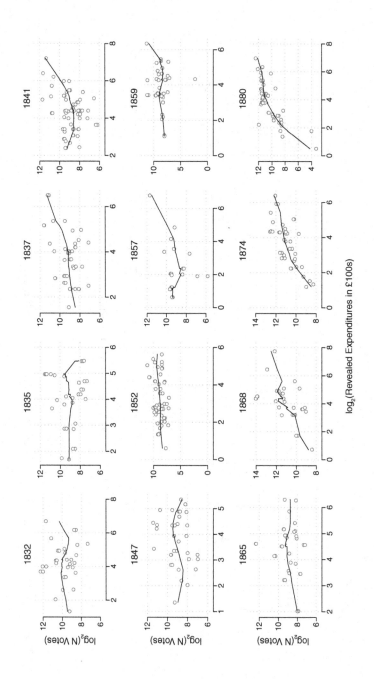

Lowess bandwidth = .8

Expenditures are denominated in 1906 GDP–deflated terms

Figure 3.4 The relationship between candidates' revealed expenditures and their vote totals at contested elections, 1857–1886.

incumbents raise and spend money in response to the strength of the challenger (see, e.g., Green and Krasno 1988; Jacobson 1990; Levitt 1994). Estimating the marginal effect of money on electoral outcomes thus requires us to control for a candidate's expectation of their own electoral strength and their opponent's expenditure, and vice versa.

We deal with these complications by focusing our attention on contested elections in which the number of Conservative and Liberal candidates was identical, and in which no independent candidates ran.[14] These were elections in which candidates of each party presumably held roughly equal prospects of victory. We then compute two quantities:

1. The Conservative–Liberal "vote gap" (VOTE GAP) – that is, the aggregate percentage of the vote won by the Conservative candidates minus the aggregate percentage of the vote won by the Liberal candidates.
2. The Conservative–Liberal "spending gap" (SPEND GAP) – that is, the amount the Conservative candidates jointly spent minus the amount the Liberal candidates jointly spent, denominated in £100s. To ensure that the spending gap does not merely reflect variation in the availability of spending data, we limit our analysis to elections for which published spending figures are available for all candidates.

We estimate the marginal effect of campaign spending on votes by regressing the vote gap on the spending gap:

$$VOTE\ GAP_{jt} = \beta_0 + \beta_1 SPEND\ GAP_{jt} + \beta_k \sum X_{jt} + e_{jt} \qquad (3.4)$$

where X is a vector of control variables, and where β_1 provides our estimate of the marginal effect of campaign spending on votes. The subscripts denote constituency j at election t. We include two variables in X: the Conservative–Liberal "incumbent gap" (INCUMBENT GAP) – that is, the difference in the number of Conservative and Liberal incumbents seeking re-election in the constituency; and BIAS. Both of these variables control for nonmonetary factors that presumably gave one party an electoral advantage over the other.

We estimate three specifications of Equation 3.4 via OLS (see Table 3.1). The first is estimated on the pooled data without regard to constituency or election fixed effects. This specification returns an estimate of β_1 of 0.19, implying that that a £100 increase in the Conservative–Liberal spending gap is associated with a 0.19 percent increase in the Conservative–Liberal vote gap. The estimate of β_1 remains steady at 0.21 when election fixed effects are added to the model

---

[14] We classify Liberal Unionists at the 1886 election as Conservatives, but we exclude any election in which there was a mixture of Liberal Unionist and Conservative candidates.

Table 3.1 Regression of Conservative-Liberal vote gaps on Conservative-Liberal spending gaps at parliamentary elections, 1857–1906

	OLS			IV (LIML)	
	1	**2**	**3**	**4**	**5**
SPEND GAP$_{jt}$ (in £100s)	0.19†	0.21†	0.27†	0.41**	0.30
	(0.06)	(0.05)	(0.07)	(0.20)	(0.20)
INCUMBENT GAP$_{jt}$	4.24†	4.29†	0.59	4.14†	4.27†
	(0.52)	(0.55)	(0.62)	(0.54)	(0.55)
BIAS$_{jt}$	27.22†	31.99†	26.74*	26.15†	31.44†
	(5.08)	(5.19)	(14.86)	(5.23)	(5.25)
CONSTANT	−13.07†	−15.11†	−13.12†	−13.26†	−6.81†
	(2.26)	(2.53)	(6.27)	(2.29)	(2.10)
Constituency fixed effects	No	No	No	No	No
Election fixed effects	No	Yes	Yes	No	Yes
N	607				
R^2	0.14	0.21	0.67	0.13	0.21
Monteil–Pfleuger effective F-statistic				12.99	12.35
% of worst-case bias				10%	10%

Subscripts denote candidate i at the election in constituency j at year t.
Cell entries are regression coefficients. Numbers in parentheses are robust standard errors.
†p <0.01 **p < 0.05 *p <0.10

(Specification 2). Replacing the election fixed effects with constituency fixed effects (Specification 3) increases the estimate of β_1 to 0.27.

To the extent that the Liberals (or Conservatives) allowed themselves to be outspent in precisely those elections where they anticipated spending to have little impact on the outcome, the spending gap is endogenous to candidates' expectations about their electoral prospects. Such a dynamic would imply that the OLS estimates of Specifications 1–3 are biased.[15] We address this concern by using the "slate gap," the district magnitude, and the logged population of the constituency as instruments for SPEND GAP. We discuss the formation of slates (i.e., alliances of copartisans in multimember constituencies) in the next

---

[15] The bias could be upward or downward depending on whether the Liberals (Conservatives) allowed themselves to be outspent in constituencies where they anticipated they would nonetheless win, or, alternatively, in constituencies where they anticipated they would lose no matter what they spent.

section, but we note here that slates can be identified from the published accounts that candidates submitted. The slate gap consists of the number of Conservative slates contesting the election in a given constituency minus the number of Liberal slates contesting the same election. This variable takes on just three values: +1 when the Conservatives are organized as a slate and the Liberals are not, 0 when neither or both sides are organized as slates, and −1 when the Liberals are organized as a slate and the Conservatives are not.

To the extent that the chief benefit of running as a slate was to provide candidates with an economy of scale in campaign spending (as we argue in the next section), the slate gap should effect the vote gap only through the spending gap. Put differently, given that the vote gap consists of the difference in the aggregate Conservative vote share minus the aggregate Liberal vote share, the vote gap should not be affected directly by whether the Conservative or Liberal candidates ran as a slate or independently. Our first-stage equation is thus,

$$SPEND\ GAP_{jt} = \alpha_0 + \alpha_1 log_2 POPULATION_{jt} + \alpha_2 SLATE\ GAP_{jt} + \alpha_3 M_{jt}$$
$$+ \alpha_4 SLATE\ GAP \times M_{jt} + u_{jt} \tag{3.5}$$

We estimate Equations 3.4 and 3.5 simultaneously via limited information maximum likelihood.[16] The resulting estimates appear in columns 4 and 5 of Table 3.1. Specification 4 is an analog to Specification 1 in that it is estimated without regard to constituency or election fixed effects. Specification 4 returns an estimate of the spending gap coefficient of 0.41, approximately twice as large as the corresponding OLS estimate. Specification 5 adds election fixed effects to the IV model. The estimated coefficient of the spending gap declines to 0.30, but this is still substantially larger than the comparable OLS estimate of 0.21.

One generally expects IV estimates to be smaller than comparable OLS estimates. We see three possible reasons for why this is not the case here. First, our instruments may be weak. The Montiel–Pflueger test statistics

---

[16] Estimating 3.5 via OLS provides,

$$SPEND\ GAP_{jt} = -\underset{(5.98)}{20.58} - \underset{(0.37)}{1.60 log_2}\ POPULATION_{jt} - \underset{(12.44)}{43.17}\ SLATE\ GAP_{jt}$$

$$-\underset{(0.77)}{0.33 M_{jt}} + \underset{(5.98)}{20.82}\ SLATE\ GAP \times M_{jt}$$

N=634 R_2 =0.08 F(4, 629)=9.37
Robust standard errors in parentheses.*p <0.10 ** p <0.05 † p <0.01

indicate that the bias in our IV estimates is 10 percent at worst, however.[17] Second, the assumption that the instruments affect the vote gap only via the spending gap may not hold. That is a risk with IV models, and it cannot be tested. A third possibility, however, is that the OLS coefficients are biased downward because candidates systematically underreported their true spending. Underreporting of this sort would impose an errors-in-variables bias on the OLS estimates that would be purged from the IV estimates.

It is helpful to place these marginal effects in context. The interquartile range of the spending gap is approximately £500. A spending gap of this size in favor of the Conservatives is associated with a vote advantage over the Liberals of between 1.0 and 2.0 percent depending on the specification. The lower bound of this estimate exceeded the margin of votes between the last-winning candidate and the first-losing candidate at approximately 10 percent of contested elections, and the upper bound at approximately 20 percent of contested elections. Victorian-era politicians and voters were not entirely mistaken in their belief that elections rested on which side spent most.

3.2.2 The Marginal Effect of Money on Votes Over Time

We can get some sense of how the marginal effect of campaign spending on electoral outcomes evolved over time by including a set of interactions between the Conservative–Liberal spending gap and a set of election period dummies in Equation 3.4. The results of this exercise are expressed visually in Figure 3.5.

Figure 3.5 shows an initial and sharp decline in the marginal effect of spending on votes in 1865. The Conservative–Liberal vote gap at the 1857 and 1859 elections increased by 2 percent for every £100 by which the Conservatives candidates outspent their Liberal opponents. Between 1865 and 1880, however, every £100 of "outspending" was associated with increase in the vote gap of at most 0.5 percent; it may have had no effect whatsoever at the 1865 and 1868 elections. The marginal effect of spending on votes recovered, however, and by 1886 it was the same as it had been in 1859.

The marginal effect of spending on votes at the 1886 elections was not due to widespread electoral corruption; the electorate was much too large for that. Evidence instead suggests that money played an increasingly important role in voter mobilization after the Third Reform Act. First, the resurgence in the marginal effect of spending on votes followed almost immediately after the extension of the franchise in 1884 via the Third Reform Act. Second, from 1885 onward, candidates spent an increasing fraction of their budgets on campaign

---

[17] Our instruments are, however, too weak to support constituency fixed effects or election period-spending gap interactions.

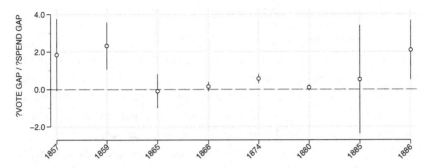

Figure 3.5 The marginal effect of the Conservative–Liberal spending gap on Conservative–Liberal vote gap at each general election held between 1857 and 1886.

literature and advertising that was designed to encourage voter turnout (Rix 2016). Third, if we regress voter turnout on the spending gap, we find a strong negative relationship between the spending gap and turnout for the 1885 and 1886 elections, but no relationship whatsoever for previous elections.[18]

Even so, the unusual nature of the 1886 election – brought about just months after the 1885 election because of the Liberal government's collapse over Home Rule for Ireland – suggests caution in ascribing the recovery of the marginal effect of money on votes to any single cause. Regardless of the precise reasons for this recovery, it demonstrates that money still exerted a significant effect on electoral outcomes at English elections even after average levels of campaign expenditures had declined.

---

[18] The regression model is,

$$TURNOUT_{jt} = \beta_0 + \beta_1 SPEND\ GAP_{jt} + \sum \tau_t T + u_{jt,}$$

where $TURNOUT_{jt}$ is the turnout at the election in constituency j at election t, and $\sum \tau_t T_t$ is a set of election fixed effects. For elections of 1885 and 1886, we obtain,

$$TURNOUT_{jt} = 82.12 - 0.44\ SPEND\ GAP_{jt} + \sum \tau_t T.$$
$$\quad\quad\quad\quad (0.72)\quad (0.28)$$

N = 126 R^2 = 0.11

For the elections previous to 1885, we obtain,

$$TURNOUT_{jt} = 82.64 - 0.04\ SPEND\ GAP_{jt} + \sum \tau_t T$$
$$\quad\quad\quad\quad (0.45)\quad (0.04)$$

N = 476 R^2 = 0.03

Numbers in parentheses are robust standard errors.

3.3 Budget Constraints

Average electioneering expenditures increased by between £500 to £1,000 starting in 1865. Whether or not the magnitude of these changes was sufficient to induce candidates to alter their electoral strategies and overhaul their campaign organizations is nonetheless unclear. In theory, the pressure on candidates to adopt cheaper programmatic electoral strategies mounted as the cost of electioneering by traditional methods closed in on the amounts that they could afford to spend. Conversely, if most candidates were exceedingly wealthy, an increase of £1,000 in the average cost of a contested election would have had little impact on how they fought elections.

There is evidence that financial concerns made MPs amenable to anticorruption legislation. W. H. Smith, for example, observed that his Conservative colleagues' acceptance of the strict spending limits of the 1883 Corrupt and Illegal Practices Act was motivated by financial pressure not principled agreement:

> I should wish to retain the power of fighting elections by paid agency if necessary as in the past: – but I am afraid I am in a small minority in the Party in the House of Commons – who only think of one thing – lessening the cheque to be drawn on their bankers. (quoted in Hanham 1959, 247)

We can gain insight into candidates' financial circumstances by examining the value at probate of the estates of deceased candidates. Supplementing the data originally collected by W. O. Aydelotte (1966) provides us with estate values for 542 candidates, of whom 474 served in the House of Commons. Aydelotte coded the probate values categorically, and we maintain his coding scheme to aid comparability. The probate values are also denominated in nominal terms, but the amounts below can be put into context by noting that an estate of £100,000 would represent between £35–70 million in 2020 terms.

Figure 3.6 shows the distribution of these probate values among candidates who first stood for election before and after 1868. While our sample is small, it conforms to Rubinstein's (1981, 167–168) observation that the membership of the House of Commons was substantially wealthier in the latter half of the nineteenth century than it had been earlier in the century. More than 60 percent of the candidates in the 1868–1880 period left behind estates valued at £50,000 or more, as compared to 49 percent of the candidates in the 1832–1867 period. Thus, while many candidates were easily wealthy enough to absorb £2,000 per election, there existed a sizable minority for whom the increased cost of elections would have been burdensome. The increase in the cost of electioneering from 1865 onward was certainly large enough relative to the latter group's financial resources to push them to look for cheaper ways to fight elections, but such incentives cannot have pressed so keenly on wealthier candidates.

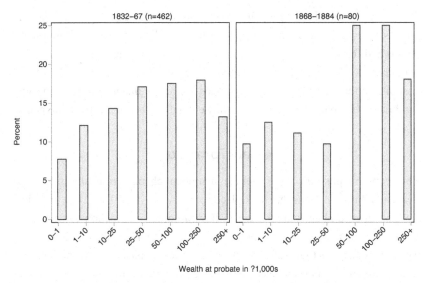

Figure 3.6 Value at probate of candidates' estates, 1832–1867 and 1868–1880.

3.4 Conclusion

The fixed costs associated with a contested election increased sharply in 1865. The marginal effect of money on votes declined at the same time. There were two proximate causes for these changes. First, the percentage of contested constituencies increased from 45 percent in 1859 to 56 percent in 1865. Second, candidates at the 1865 election contested larger constituencies than in the recent past. The average electorate of contested constituencies at the three general elections of the 1850s was 3,157 voters; in 1865, it was 3,567. Some part of this difference was due to the natural growth of the electorate, but it also reflected a greater willingness on the part of Liberal candidates to contest county constituencies. This was, in turn, related to the long-run social and economic changes that were making the party system friendlier to Liberal candidates. The expansion of the electorate in 1868 amplified all of these effects, but it did not cause them.

The timing of these changes also points to a deeper causal force – that is, the resumption in earnest of two-party competition. The break-up of the Conservatives in 1847 over the repeal of the Corn Laws had left the party system in a state of confusion, depriving the elections of the 1850s of clarity and decisiveness. By 1865, however, the last of the Peelites had either retired from politics or joined the Liberal ranks (Conacher 1972; Gurowich 1984). The decline in the split-voting rate from 19 percent in 1857 to 8.5 percent in 1865 (Cox 1987, 103) reflected a return to two-party competition.

The next section investigates how these political changes combined with the increasing cost of electioneering to alter how candidates organized their campaigns and fought elections. We should not overstate the economic pressure on candidates to adopt programmatic campaign strategies, however. The increased cost of elections after 1865 certainly imposed a heavy financial burden on some candidates, but many others were wealthy enough to absorb the greater expense.

4 Slate Formation

The economic position of the average incumbent changed radically in the nine years and three elections that took place between 1859 and 1868. The probability that an incumbent would have to fight a contested election to secure re-election to the House of Commons had jumped from.45 in 1859 to.76 in 1868. The incumbent was thus half as likely as in the recent past to enjoy the financial respite of an uncontested election. The extension of the suffrage in 1868 increased the expected cost of that re-election bid from approximately £520 in 1859 to £1,200 in 1868. The marginal effect of that spending on election outcomes had also collapsed. In 1859, outspending an opponent by £100 generated an electoral advantage of up 2 percent of the vote; by 1868, a similar sum secured an advantage of just.15 percent.

This was an opportune time for parties and candidates to rethink how to fund, organize, and contest elections – and to a degree they did. Starting in the 1870s, the Conservative and Liberal parties began to establish central party organizations to coordinate voter registration, candidate selection, and fund raising. Related organizations (e.g., the Conservative National Union and the National Liberal Federation) were developed to link the party organizations in the constituencies to the central party (Hanham 1959; Kuo 2018; Rix 2016). This was a fitful process, however. It was 1900 before the central parties could reliably subsidize their candidates and produce and disseminate the bulk of party literature (Rix 2016). At the constituency level, caucuses of activists began to wrest control of candidate selection and local campaigns from local notables (Ostrogorski 1902), but this, too, was a slow process; by 1880, there were Liberal caucuses in just 77 of 282 constituencies (Rix 2016).

However, as we show in this section, coordination and consolidation were already emerging in the constituencies in the form of coalitions or slates (we use the terms interchangeably) – that is, organizational alliances between two candidates of the same party. The central argument is that the formation of party slates was held back by what we call a *financial free-rider problem*. The chief obstacle to forming a slate was the concern that each candidate would make a large financial contribution to a joint campaign only to find that his money worked mainly to get his running mate elected. This financial free-rider problem was largely resolved by a party-oriented electorate. Once the electorate voted along party lines, a candidate could be assured that any vote that went to his running mate would be accompanied by a second vote for himself.

The formation of party slates relates to a series of theoretical and empirical puzzles. The first is a theoretical puzzle regarding the nature of party organization. To function and maintain themselves, parties must eliminate free-riding on the party label and elicit costly effort from candidates in the absence of guaranteed selective benefits (Aldrich 1995; Kam 2009; Schlesinger 1984). The fact that the Liberals defeated their own governments in 1834, 1866, and 1886, and that the Tories broke their party apart in 1847, indicates that shared ideology was on its own insufficient to overcome these problems. To an extent, these collective action problems operate independently of ideology.

A second puzzle concerns the theoretical mechanism by which three-cornered contests gave way to four-candidate races in which two Liberals confronted two Conservatives. Cox (1987, 138) argues that party orientation was necessary and sufficient for this transition: given a highly party-oriented electorate, a constituency that was electorally propitious for one Conservative (Liberal) was equally propitious for a second Conservative (Liberal). What Cox's explanation ignores, and what we highlight, is the strategic importance of the financial and organizational aspects of the campaign. A second Conservative entrant not only had to worry that his two Liberal opponents had formed a slate that allowed them to outspend him, he also had to worry that his Conservative copartisan would free-ride on his financial contributions to any joint campaign. This is not an arcane point. The resolution of these collective action problems transformed local campaigns from personal into partisan organizations, and the emergence of two-versus-two races imparted a partisan uniformity to local elections across the country. This was a crucial step in the development of electoral competition that was uniformly partisan in complexion and national in scope.

A third puzzle relates to the pace at which party organization emerged and the process by which it did so. Kuo (2018) and Ziblatt (2017) argue (albeit from different perspectives) that British party organizations emerged as a function of party leaders' efforts to build centrally directed hierarchical structures. These centralizing efforts, moreover, accelerated after the 1868 Reform Act and were only fully established well after the 1885 Reform Act (Rix 2016). Cox is ambivalent as to whether the parties' organizational efforts were top-down or bottom-up, but his analysis of trends in party organization is heavily reliant on an 1874 census of Conservative party associations (Cox 1987). In contrast, we show that the formation of party slates at local elections accelerated from 1857 onwards. The transformation of local campaigns from personal into partisan organizations thus began well before the 1868 Reform Act, and emerged organically as a function of the constituency electorate's party orientation. In other words, there was significant intraparty coordination within constituencies well in advance of the 1868 Reform Act.

The section follows in four parts. Part 4.1 uses qualitative and quantitative data to chart the change in candidates' attitudes and their campaign organizations over time. Part 4.2 discusses the obstacles to the formation of party slates; again, the approach is both qualitative and quantitative as we use historical cases and formal modeling to highlight the collective action problem that copartisan candidates confronted in trying to form a slate. Part 4.3 tests our argument against data, and provides statistical evidence that links slate formation to the propensity of the electorate to vote along party lines. Part 4.4 considers alternative explanations for the formation of party slates.

4.1 Parties and Slates

The change over time in attitudes toward parties and partisanship is conveyed by the language of candidates' speeches to electors. The 1837 Leominster election poll book, for example, records Lord Hotham, the Conservative incumbent, declaring in his nomination speech that:

> if he could not go [to the House of Commons] as an independent man, he had no desire to go at all. . . . He would pursue the same independent course. . . . If you will place me again in the same situation, it will be my study to uphold the just and lawful prerogatives of the Crown – the well defined powers of the Aristocracy, and the rights and liberties of the people (Chilcott 1837, 5).

The last sentence of Hotham's speech clearly identifies him as a Conservative, but he neither employs that label nor even claims a party affiliation. Hotham's opponents were similarly circumspect, though one was clearly a Liberal and the other a fellow Conservative. Furthermore, despite the presence of another Conservative candidate, and the fact that Leominster was a double-member constituency which offered voters the opportunity to vote for both Conservatives, Hotham nonetheless campaigned independently. The election was thus a three-cornered contest between two Conservatives and a lone Liberal. This was the standard practice at the time (Cox 1987, 102 n. 4). This pattern of competition reflected the customary value that was placed on political independence, a traditional understanding of parties as instruments of faction rather than representation (Scarrow 2006), and the corresponding weakness of party labels and organizations in the early decades of the nineteenth century (Newbould 1985; O'Gorman 1984).

Hotham's independence was largely a fiction, of course; candidates who claimed to be independent of party on the hustings nonetheless tended to act as loyal Liberals or Conservatives once elected to the House of Commons, and they had done so for years prior to the passage of the First Reform Act 1832 (Aydelotte 1966; Cox 1987; Eggers and Spirling 2016). The pace at which the English electorate recognized and endorsed this reality is indicated by Herbert Ingram's address to the electors of Boston in 1859. Ingram stressed that the election concerned

> the transfer of power from the present advisers of the Crown to the Liberal Party. With that party it has been my privilege and my pleasure to act – a party that in former years when in power contributed greatly to the prosperity of the nation, and with which, if again returned to Parliament by your independent suffrages, it will be my duty and my pleasure once more to co-operate. (Noble 1859, 6–7)

The contrast between Hotham's stress on independence and Ingram's proud statement of his affiliation to the Liberal Party is striking. Ingram's campaign differed from Hotham's in another important way; in contrast to Hotham, Ingram campaigned in tandem with the second Liberal candidate at Boston, Meaburn Staniland. In the language of the day, Ingram and Staniland formed a coalition; they operated a joint election committee and jointly financed the campaign. The contrast between Hotham's independence at Leominster in 1837 and Ingram and Staniland's partisan cooperation at Boston in 1859 suggests a sea change in both party organization and normative values over time.

A similar pattern emerges if we trace the configuration of electoral competition within a single constituency over time. The 1837 Middlesex election, for example, saw two Liberal candidates (Hume and Byng) oppose two Conservatives (Wood and Pownal). The Conservatives did their part to make the election a party fight, advertising in the *Morning Post* (Saturday, July 15, 1837) that a joint committee had been formed to secure the election of Wood and Pownal. The same day, however, Hume and Byng's campaigns announced that there would be no coalition between the two Liberals (*Woolmer's Exeter and Plymouth Gazette*, Saturday, July 15, 1837; pg. 4; Issue 2376).

The structure of electoral competition at Middlesex became more firmly partisan over time. At the 1874 Middlesex election, two Liberals (Enfield and Lehmann) again confronted two Conservatives (Hamilton and Coope). In contrast to 1837, however, the Liberals and Conservatives contested the election as coalitions. We know this because Enfield and Lehmann submitted a single joint account of £6,126, and Hamilton and Coope did likewise, reporting joint expenses of £10,501 (P.P. 1874 [358], 7). This indicates that the candidates on both sides funded a single electoral organization and ran as party coalitions.

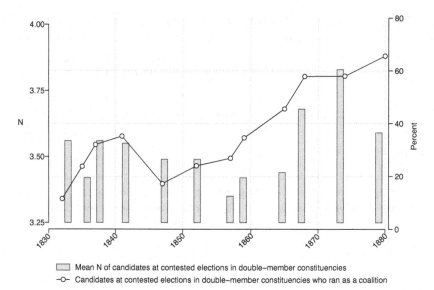

Mean N of candidates at contested elections in double–member constituencies
–o– Candidates at contested elections in double–member constituencies who ran as a coalition

Figure 4.1 Party slates and the average number of candidates at contested elections in double-member constituencies, 1832–1886.

These examples suggest that the financial and organizational basis of electoral competition changed between the 1830s and 1870s, with candidates of the same party tending to contest multimember constituencies as party slates rather than independently, as had been common in earlier years. On the basis of candidates' financial accounts and historical reports of elections from newspapers, poll books, and petitions, we are able to estimate the percentage of candidates at contested elections in double-member constituencies who ran as part of a coalition. These data appear in Figure 4.1, alongside estimates of the mean number of candidates at contested elections in double-member constituencies. Figure 4.1 shows that the percentage of candidates who ran in coalition with a copartisan declined after 1841, a direct result of the Conservative party's division over the repeal of the Corn Laws. There was a slow recovery in coalitions until the 1859 elections, whereupon there was a 10 percent spike in the percentage of candidates who ran on a coalition. A similar spike followed at the 1865 election, and from the 1868 election onward the majority of candidates in double-member contests ran on party slates.

Up until the 1865 election, the mean number of candidates at contested elections in double-member constituencies hovered around 3.4. Taken in conjunction with the relatively low proportion of coalitions, this figure indicates that up until 1865 half of the elections in double-member constituencies were three-cornered contests. The number of candidates contesting double-member constituencies then increased substantially at the 1868 and 1874 elections. The increase in the number of candidates at double-member contest constituencies thus lagged behind the propensity of candidates fighting these elections to form coalitions. As we argue below, this suggests a pattern by which two candidates on one side coalescing at one election encouraged the other side to bring in a second candidate and form a coalition at the next election. In this manner, the modal number of candidates contesting two-member constituencies increased from three to four; three-cornered contests gave way to bipartisan competition between party slates, and the nature of electoral competition evolved from personal to partisan.

4.2 Slates and Financial Free-riding

There were identifiable costs and benefits to running on a slate, and candidates weighed these carefully before agreeing to coalition with a copartisan. The standard argument for adopting a running mate was to reduce the likelihood of the candidate's own defeat. The logic is that, absent a running mate, a candidate's supporters would be tempted to give their second votes to the opposing candidate that they saw as the lesser of two evils. In this fashion, a candidate might be defeated by the second votes of his own supporters (Cox 1987, 102; Hanham 1959, 197). There was also a prevailing belief that an unpopular running mate would bring about the defeat of both candidates. The coalition between Beckett and Tempest at the 1835 Leeds election, for example, was described as having "corrosive effects" on Beckett's election prospects (*The Morning Chronicle*, January 8, 1835). Meaburn Staniland (mentioned earlier) similarly blamed his defeat at Boston in 1868 on the fact that his running mate's radicalism frightened the constituency's moderate voters (C. 1441 [1876], 242 §13078–13090).

Gash (1953, 281–295) records such dynamics at work in Reading at the 1835 and 1837 elections. Reading's vibrant dissenting community and nascent industrial sector ostensibly made it fertile ground for radicalism, but its inhabitants "were too solidly middle class and prosperous to welcome extreme measures" (Gash 1953, 285), and the borough's agricultural connections were too strong for Reading's voters to embrace free trade wholeheartedly. The more radical of Reading's Liberals nevertheless insisted on nominating extremists. This split the party, and both elections were fought by two independent Liberal committees, one whiggish and the other radical. The Conservatives matched the Liberal's disunity at the 1847 election. The two Conservatives, Russell and Chelsea, were on opposite sides of their party's free trade split and their committees issued separate advertisements (*Berkshire Chronicle*, Saturday,

July 24, 1847; pg. 1). On the Liberal side, the chairman of Talfourd's committee flatly declared that their candidate was not interested in a coalition "with a radical like Pigott" (*Berkshire Chronicle*, Saturday, July 24, 1847; pg. 2). The 1847 Reading election thus saw every candidate fend for themselves.

We do not deny the electoral logic for adopting a running mate or that ideological considerations bore on the matter. We contend, however, that financial motives played a crucial role in the selection of candidates and the formation of party alliances. The high cost of electioneering and the relative poverty of the central parties combined to make a candidate's personal wealth a principal criterion for the candidate's nomination. For example, in his testimony to a Royal Commission, Henry Westropp, a Conservative candidate for Bridgewater in 1859, recalled that the local Conservative notables had selected a Mr. Henry Padwick as Westropp's running mate for purely financial reasons:

Q: Did you know Mr. Padwick?

A: *I had never spoken to him.* In a very short time when I had came down here I had discovered that there were very sinister rumors afloat respecting Mr. Padwick. Whether true or false is not for me to say, nor do I know at this moment, but, however, they annoyed me very terribly through being mixed up with such a person about whom such things were said I wrote to Sir Fredrick Slade to ask him. He told me *that he knew nothing of him whatever, but that he could lay a continuous line of sovereigns from Bridgewater to Bristol.* That struck me as being a most exceeding forcible expression. (P.P. 1870 [C-12], 869, §34950) [our emphasis]

Having never spoken to Padwick, Westropp could not have known what Padwick's politics were. All that mattered, as Sir Fredrick Slade's (the Conservative's election agent) response to Westropp's inquiries underscored, was that Padwick was exceedingly wealthy.

The high cost of electioneering placed financial pressure on candidates to secure running mates. Electioneering costs weighed especially heavily on singleton candidates who contested double-member constituencies. Singletons had to bear single-handedly the costs of mounting an election and enjoyed no savings in the market for votes because of a widespread tendency for plumpers to cost at least twice as much as single votes. The premium cost of plumpers was common knowledge. *The Times* (1 July 1841, Issue 17711, 2, col. D), for example, explained Henry G. R. Yorke's reputed expenditure of £10,000 at the 1841 York City election by the fact that "Mr. Yorke polled no less than 1,355 plumpers, which, of course, are dearer than split votes, and may account for his vast expenditure." These circumstances placed singleton candidates at a financial disadvantage especially in contests against two copartisans who were running as a slate. And even if the marginal effect of money on votes was in decline after 1859, being outspent by a large margin condemned a candidate to defeat (see Table 3.1).

A second Liberal or Conservative candidate would appear to have had a corresponding financial incentive to run as a slate rather than run alone. The difficulty was that both candidates needed assurance that their financial contributions to the joint campaign would help to get themselves rather than their running mates elected. We refer to this as the *financial free-rider problem*. That this was a concern is indicated by the fact that nascent slates would often fall apart because one candidate's supporters would not vote for the running mate. At the 1835 Stockport election, for example, the Liberal candidates, Henry Marsland and Edward Davenport, reportedly fell out and used "very severe language towards each other" due to Marsland's supporters not splitting votes with Davenport (*Chester Chronicle and Cheshire and North Wales General Advertiser*, 23 January 1835, 3). Under such conditions, finances were predictably a source of tension between copartisans. At Northamptonshire South, for example, "[Henry] Cartwright's election debts proved an enduring problem over the subsequent decade [the 1850s and '60s], causing increasing tension between himself and [Rainald] Knightley as the latter became wary of shouldering the burden of the Conservative interest in the division."[19]

Political parties at this time were agglomerations of like-minded individuals. As such, parties were vulnerable to internal disagreements, not only over national issues such as religious toleration, free trade, and Ireland, but also over local matters, such as whether an aristocratic family's interest afforded them a legitimate claim on both of a constituency's seats. In this context, and without any outside actor to coordinate and enforce agreements (e.g., a central party hierarchy), the question of how a joint campaign would be organized and funded was a vexing one. Coalitions were always vulnerable to defection because of the real possibility that one member would get elected while the other suffered defeat. The breakdown of the Liberal coalition at the 1832 election in Essex South is illustrative of this danger:

> After the first day of polling, Hall Dare [the Conservative candidate] had a commanding lead of nearly 500 votes, leaving the contest between the two Reformers. Wellesley's wife subsequently instructed her husband's supporters to plump for him on the second day, a missive that prompted Lennard's supporters to retaliate and only back their man. Although Wellesley gained majorities in his own strongholds of Romford and

---

[19] www.historyofparliamentonline.org/volume/1832–1868/constituencies/northamptonshire-south. Accessed January 15, 2018. Interested readers should contact the History of Parliament Trust for access.

Epping, he was outpolled elsewhere, and Lennard was elected in second place, by a margin of 106 votes. Wellesley, as was his custom, immediately sought to lay blame, castigating the local Whigs for a breach of faith. They in turn accused him of abandoning the coalition at the first sign of trouble.[20]

We find even more compelling evidence that copartisan candidates confronted a financial free-riding problem in the fact that candidates sometimes took the trouble to write contingent contracts specifying how the electioneering costs and parliamentary seats were to be shared between them. An elaborate example of a contingent contract of this sort is provided by the 1847 election for the western division of Somersetshire. The agents of the two Liberal candidates, Bickham Escott and P. P. Bouverie, signed a memorandum of understanding, initialed in the margins by the candidates, that stated:

> The Honorable Philip Playdell Bouverie and Bickham Escott, Esq, Candidates.
>
> For the purpose of securing the Election of the above named Candidates it is agreed by the respective committees on their behalf that the Expense of the Election shall be borne by each of the Candidates in the following manner, viz. in case one thousand Electors (more or less) shall split their votes for "Bouverie and Escott" the expense of bringing such Electors to the Poll and of refreshments for those Electors afterwards shall be borne and paid by and between the above named candidates equally. But the expense of bringing to the Poll any Electors who may split their votes for "Bouverie and Hood" or "Bouverie and Moody" shall be borne solely by Mr Bouverie and the Expense of bringing to the Poll any Elector who may split their votes for "Escott and Hood" or "Escott and Moody" shall be borne solely by Mr Escott.
>
> It is further agreed that the Expense of the Committee Rooms and Check clerks and any other Expenses incidental to the Committee Rooms shall be borne equally between Mr Bouverie and Mr Escott. At this Eleventh day of August 1847. (SO Record Office, DD/SF 13/3/16)

The agreement did not end well. Correspondence between Escott and his agent indicates that Escott found the agreement to be highly unsatisfactory ex post. In an angry letter, Escott charged that he was being asked to pay more than agreed, and that if there were "any intelligible reason why I should pay part of Mr Bouverie's debts on account of that contest I never heard such reason stated." Escott felt that Mr Bouverie's agents had taken advantage of him. Escott closed the letter by declaring flatly that he "refuse[d] to pay one shilling more."

---

[20] www.historyofparliamentonline.org/volume/1832–1868/constituencies/essex-south. Accessed January 15, 2018.

Another example of a contingent contract comes from the 1852 election at Hull, where the two Liberal candidates, Lord Goderich and James Clay (the incumbent), signed a formal agreement to "run in harness" – i.e., form a slate. The terms of the agreement stipulated that:

> That Lord Goderich pays the first £1,000 expenses. That above £1,000 Mr. Clay pays half the expenses up to the sum of £3,000, inclusive of the first £1,000, beyond which amount it is agreed that the expenses shall not go. That the above expenses commence, except that they include the street lists, from Monday next June 14th. (P.P. 1854 [1703], xiii)

This agreement proved unenforceable: an investigation revealed that Goderich and Clay's expenses came to £5,955 – almost twice their agreed limit! The Escott–Bouverie and Goderich–Clay agreements are exceptional only in their written formality; the Liberal candidates at Gloucester in 1859 (P.P. 1860 [2586], 169, §7035) and the Conservatives at Chester in 1881 (C. 1881 [2824], xii) struck verbal agreements of a similar nature.

The collective action problem that potential running mates confronted was exacerbated by the fact that candidates tended to be transient. Losing candidates had good reasons to search for more promising constituencies. Incumbents also frequently decamped to safer seats (Coates and Dalton 1992). The churn of candidates across seats meant that 68 percent of slates were one-time relationships. Reputational concerns or a fear of retaliation were unlikely to have been sufficiently strong in such an environment to induce candidates to live up to their financial obligations.

In theory, the financial free-rider problem was easier to overcome in highly party-oriented constituencies. A highly party-oriented electorate addressed both sides' concerns in this way: If party-oriented voters voted for the party and not for the individual candidates, then any running mate willing to contribute financially was politically satisfactory from the incumbent singleton's perspective. Similarly, if party-oriented voters voted for the party and not for the individual candidates, then the entering candidate could be assured that votes would, in fact, not just flow to his running mate but to him as well. A party-oriented electorate resolved copartisans' collective action problem.

4.3 A Model of Slate Formation

Formalizing this argument makes our claim more explicit. Assume that candidates value a parliamentary seat at $S > 0$ and that the probability of winning the election is proportional to their spending such that in a three-cornered contest, candidate i's expected utility is:

$$EU_i(independent) = \frac{K_i}{\sum_{i=1}^{3} K_i} S - K_i - F, \tag{4.1}$$

where K_i is candidate i's spending, and F is the fixed cost of contesting the election. Assume also that candidate i and j are of the same party and form a coalition that allows them to split the fixed cost of contesting the election and pool their spending. The extent to which j's spending spills over to i's benefit (and vice versa) hinges on the party orientation of the constituency's electorate, $\rho \in [0, 1]$. Equally, the coalition leaves i vulnerable to moral hazard on j's side (e.g., j may renege on his contribution) such that i ends up bearing $(1 + c)$, $c > 0$, of the cost of the campaign. The coalition thus provides i with an expected utility of:

$$EU_i(coalition) = \frac{K_i + \rho K_j}{\sum_{i=1}^{3} K_i} S - (1 + c)K_i - \frac{F}{2}. \tag{4.2}$$

Elementary algebra shows that i prefers to run in coalition with j rather than independently if and only if:

$$\frac{\rho K_j}{\sum_{i=1}^{3} K_i} S > cK_i - \frac{F}{2}. \tag{4.3}$$

Equation 4.3 shows that slate formation was contingent on the electorate's party orientation, ρ, in as much as it would have been difficult on this model for slates to have formed in constituencies where the electorate exhibited little party orientation and ρ tended to zero. In contrast, the more party-oriented voters and higher fixed costs of elections that characterized the 1860s made coalitions more likely to emerge.

4.4 Testing the Cost-sharing and Credible Commitment Argument

The central implication of our argument is that candidates of the same party should have been more (less) likely to run as a slate in a multi-member constituency the more (less) party-oriented the constituency's electorate. Our argument also implies that there was an economy of scale to running in coalition (i.e., they could spend less individually and more jointly); absent such an advantage, there was no obvious economic incentive to run in coalition and the financial free-rider problem that we have described was moot. We first examine the relationship between split voting and the formation of copartisan coalitions, and then consider the financial implications of forming a coalition.

Our dependent variable, SLATE, indicates whether candidates of a given party operated as a slate (1) or not (0). The party orientation of a given constituency's electorate is the key causal variable in our argument. We measure the party orientation of a constituency in the same fashion as Cox – that is, via the proportion of split votes cast at an election (SV); the higher the electorate's party orientation, the lower the proportion of split votes. All else equal, then, we expect a negative relationship between slate formation and split-voting rates

We appreciate that the rate of split voting at a given election was a cause and an effect of candidates' coalition arrangements. Consequently, in some of the specifications that follow we use the split-voting rate at the last contested election in the constituency as an instrument for SV. Our models also include the constituency's structural bias and its square (BIAS and $BIAS^2$) to control for the competitiveness of the constituency; the density (DENSITY) and size of the constituency's electorate (ELECTORS), which affected the cost of contesting the constituency; and the number of other copartisans that entered the election (COPARTISANS) In general, COPARTISANS equals 1, implying that candidate A of party k is joined in constituency j at t by a single copartisan. However, there are cases in which two or more copartisans entered a constituency. Such situations offered the candidates of party k more opportunities to form a slate, but they also created the potential for coordination problems to emerge.

4.4.1 Estimation Strategy

Our resulting linear probability model can be written as:

$$Pr\big(SLATE_{kjt} = 1\big) = \theta_0 + \theta_1 SV_{jt} + \theta_2 BIAS_{jt} + \theta_3 BIAS^2_{jt} + \theta_4 log_2 ELECTORS_{jt}$$

$$+\theta_5 DENSITY_{jt} + \theta_6 INCUMBENTS_{kjt}$$

$$+\theta_7 COPARTISANS_{kjt} + u_{kjt,} \tag{4.4}$$

where the subscripts identify the candidates of party k at the election in constituency j at time t. The expectation is that $\theta_1 < 0$. Equation 4.4 is estimated across Liberal and Conservative campaigns in contested multimember constituencies in which the candidates of party k had an opportunity to run as a member of a slate (i.e., where at least one other copartisan entered the election). Thus, an election contested by two Liberal candidates and two Conservatives contributes two records: one noting whether the Liberals ran as a slate or independently, the other noting the same information for the Conservatives.[21]

---

[21] As written, the model implies that there are no differences in coalition incentives and arrangements across parties. One can relax this assumption by adding a party dummy to the model, but

4.5 Results

4.5.1 Split Voting and Slate Formation

Our estimates of Equation 4.4 are shown in Table 4.1. The first three specifications of the model are estimated via OLS. The negative coefficient of SV_{jt} in these first three specifications is in line with the prediction that higher levels of split voting (i.e., lower levels of party orientation) discouraged candidates of the same party from running as a slate. The coefficient ranges from -1.77 to -1.51, depending on the inclusion of election and constituency fixed effects in the model. These figures imply that every percentage point increase in the split-voting rate was associated with a decrease in the probability of copartisan candidates running as a slate of between 0.016 and 0.015. The interquartile range of the split-voting rate was approximately 12 percent. A decline in the split-voting rate of that magnitude would increase the probability of a slate forming by about 0.20, a large effect relative to the baseline probability of a slate forming of 0.46.

We also note that coalitions were more likely to form in constituencies with large electorates. The estimates indicate that doubling the electorate increased the probability of copartisans forming a coalition by at least 0.05, and perhaps by as much as 0.11. Again, this represents a large effect relative to the baseline probability of a slate forming.

As we noted, the split-voting rate at a given election was as much an effect of candidates' coalition arrangements as a cause. This is because once two copartisans formed a slate, they would jointly work to convince voters to cast both their votes for the slate (although, as we related earlier, such arrangements sometimes fell apart). We address this problem by using the split-voting rate at the last contested election in the constituency, SV_{jt-m}, as an instrument for SV_{jt} and estimating Equation 4.4 via limited information maximum likelihood (LIML). The LIML estimates shown in Specifications 4–6 are approximately twice as large as the OLS estimates, with a one percentage point increase in the split-voting rate implying a decrease in the probability of copartisan candidates running as a slate of approximately 0.03.

Our LIML estimates are robust to the inclusion of election fixed effects, suggesting that the relationship we document is not driven by common changes in slate formation or split voting over time. Our instruments are substantially weakened when we add constituency fixed effects to the

---

doing so has no substantive impact on the results. A less obvious assumption is that the Liberal and Conservative candidates made their slate arrangements independently.

Table 4.1 Linear probability model of party slates forming in double-member constituencies

	OLS			LIML			Proxy		
	1	2	3	4	5	6	7	8	9
SV_{jt}	-1.85†	-1.58†	-1.80†	-3.45†	-3.36†	-2.90†	-1.08†	-0.39	-0.88†
	(0.18)	(0.23)	(0.19)	(0.63)	(0.67)	(0.79)	(0.18)	(0.25)	(0.18)
$COPARTISANS_{kjt}$	-0.06*	-0.06	0.01	0.02	0.04	0.04	-0.16†	-0.19†	-0.13†
	(0.03)	(0.04)	(0.03)	(0.09)	(0.08)	(0.08)	(0.04)	(0.05)	(0.04)
$log_2ELECTORS_{jt}$	0.07†	0.10†	0.05†	0.04**	0.04*	0.05**	0.08†	0.11†	0.09†
	(0.01)	(0.02)	(0.01)	(0.02)	(0.02)	(0.02)	(0.01)	(0.03)	(0.01)
$BIAS_{jt}$	-0.52	-0.50	0.70	-0.76	1.92*	2.36**	0.43	-0.26	0.85
	(0.59)	(1.11)	(0.65)	(0.87)	(0.99)	(1.11)	(0.68)	(1.07)	(0.86)
$BIAS_{jt}^2$	0.15	-0.54	-0.97	-1.20	-1.90*	-2.50**	-1.07	-0.83	-1.18
	(0.60)	(1.20)	(0.64)	(0.89)	(0.97)	(1.11)	(0.68)	(1.18)	(0.84)
CONSTANT	-0.25			0.22			-0.10		
	(0.19)			(0.29)			(0.23)		
Constituency fixed effects	No	Yes	No	No	No	No	No	Yes	No
Election fixed effects	No	No	Yes	No	Yes	Yes	No	No	Yes
Additional controls	No	No	No	No	No	Yes	No	No	Yes
N observations		783			496			779	
R^2	0.35	0.57	0.38	0.26	0.31	0.36	0.24	0.49	0.31
Monteil–Pfleuger Effective F-statistic				51.53	53.17	41.60			
% of worst-case bias				5%<	5%<	5%<			

Cell entries are regression coefficients with robust standard errors in parentheses.

*p <0.10 **p <0.05 †p <0.01

model, however. The chief problem is that split-voting rates were only sporadically reported in newspapers and poll books, so we have only a few constituencies where the time series of split-voting rates exceeds four data points. These data points, moreover, are not always from consecutive elections. Thus, even when SV_{jt} is observed, SV_{jt-m} may not be. This explains the sharp drop-off in the number of observations between Specifications 1–3 and 4–6, and why our LIML estimates are not robust to the inclusion of constituency fixed effects.

We adopt two strategies to deal with this issue. First, we add dummy variables for the constituency's region and borough-county status in an effort to control for unobserved constituency-specific factors (Specification 6). The addition of these covariates reduces the magnitude of the SV_{jt} coefficient to –2.90, but it does not substantively alter our results. Second, we employ the lagged split-voting rate, SV_{jt-m}, as a direct proxy for SV_{jt} and estimate Equation 4.4 via OLS (Specifications 7–9).

Specification 8 is most usefully compared to Specification 2 as both include constituency fixed effects. Using SV_{jt-m} as a proxy for SV_{jt} decreases the magnitude of the coefficient on split voting from –1.58 to just –0.39. This indicates that the impact of the decline in split voting on slate formation was far more modest than suggested by the other estimates. A comparison of Specifications 6 and 9 shows the same pattern, with the coefficient on split voting declining from –2.90 to –0.88. The fact that the specifications returning the smallest coefficient estimates include constituency fixed effects suggests to us that the formation of slates was contingent not only on the split-voting rate but also on unobserved constituency-specific factors. While the coefficient estimate on split voting in Specification 8 is not statistically significant by conventional standards, it remains negative and is almost 50 percent larger than its standard error ($t = -1.56$).

4.5.2 Additional Implications

The Financial Returns

Table 4.2 provides information on the financial impact of running as a slate or independently, setting out the average electioneering expenditures (in 1906 GDP-deflated terms) per candidate in double-member constituencies contingent on the configuration of the election contest. For example, in a three-candidate contest in which one candidate ran independently and the other two ran as a slate – i.e. 2 v. 1 – we see that the independent candidate in such contests reported to Parliament an average expenditure of £1,348, as compared to £810 apiece for the two partners.

Table 4.2 Election spending in contested double-member boroughs, 1820–1906

Configuration of Competition	Published Expenditures			Revealed Expenditure		
	Mean	se	N	Mean	se	N
Ran independently						
1 v. 1 v. 1	1,162	91	271	2,213	292	64
2 v. 1	2,711	185	192	3,547	631	37
2 v. 1 v. 1	1,662	211	51	1,995	561	7
Ran as a slate						
2 v. 1	1,693	103	195	2,063	303	37
2 v. 1 v. 1	1,240	157	58	1,122	352	4
2 v. 2	1,703	48	375	1,722	142	82

The data in Table 4.2 show that running as a slate offered candidates an economy of scale and a significant electoral advantage. This is most evident with regard to the revealed figures, but the published ones tell much the same story. In a three-candidate race where all candidates ran individually, revealed spending averaged £2,213. If two candidates were able to form a slate and turn the election into a 2 v. 1 contest, however, their individual spending would decline to £2,063 (a savings of £150 apiece) whilst their joint spending would climb to £4,126. The two partners would thus enjoy a spending advantage of just shy of £580 over their singleton rival. As we demonstrated in Section 3, the electoral advantage that a £580 spending gap represented was significant. In the long term, such unbalanced contests cannot have been in equilibrium. Not only did the two copartisan candidates enjoy significant savings by running as a slate, their cooperation put financial and electoral pressure on their independent opponent. Once this occurred, the independent candidate had a strong financial incentive to secure a running mate. The spending patterns in Table 4.2 are thus consistent with our argument.

The Electoral Returns

One effect of the financial advantages of running as a slate was to restructure electoral competition along two-Liberal-versus-two-Conservative lines, and, by dint of that, to reinforce the partisan nature of electoral competition. Once that happened, one would expect one slate to win both seats. Figure 4.2 shows the percentage of contested elections in double-member constituencies at which the candidates of one party swept both seats. Consistent with our argument, it

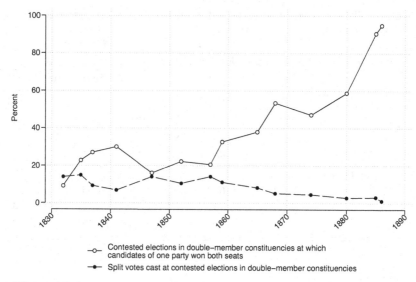

Figure 4.2 Party sweeps and split voting at double-member constituencies, 1832–1880.

increased over time at the same pace at which candidates formed coalitions (see Figure 4.1).

Figure 4.2 does not establish that candidates who organized themselves into slates enjoyed an electoral advantage relative to those who ran independently. (Rising party orientation on its own could have generated both party slates and party sweeps, and, as Figure 4.2 shows, split voting declined as sweeps increased.) However, we can directly assess and compare the electoral performance of candidates on slates to those who ran independently by examining the rank order in which candidates polled (i.e., 1st, 2st, etc.) in multimember constituencies. If slates offered candidates an electoral advantage, then candidates on slates should tend to outperform lone candidates, all else equal. We test this argument by regressing the rank order in which candidates polled ($RANK_{ijt}$) in contested elections in double-member constituencies on two dummy variables indicating whether or not the candidate in question (1) ran as part of a slate (ON_{ijt}) and (2) contended against a slate (VS_{ijt}), respectively, controlling for the number of candidates at the election ($NCANDIDATES_{jt}$). The model is

$$RANK_{ijt} = \alpha_0 + \alpha_1 ON_{ijt} + \alpha_2 VS_{ijt} + \alpha_3 NCANDIDATES_{jt} + \sum \tau_t T_t + \sum \delta_j D_j \tag{4.5}$$

where $\sum \tau_t T_t$ and $\sum \delta_j D_j$ are sets of election and constituency fixed effects, respectively. If slates offered candidates an electoral advantage, we should observe $\alpha_1 < 0$ and $\alpha_2 > 0$.

Estimating Equation 4.5 via OLS provides the following results:

$$RANK_{ijt} = \underset{(0.11)}{0.62^\dagger} - \underset{(0.04)}{0.31^\dagger ON_{ijt}} + \underset{(0.04)}{0.28^\dagger VS_{ijt}} + \underset{(0.03)}{0.47^\dagger NCANDIDATES_{jt}}$$

$$+ \sum \tau_t T_t + \sum \delta_j D_j$$

N=5,180 R^2=0.10

Robust standard errors in parentheses. $*p < 0.10$ $**p < 0.05$ $\dagger p < 0.01$

One can interpret the results as follows. The average rank order in which a candidate finished was 0.62 (the constant) plus 0.47 for every additional candidate that contested the election. With four candidates contesting an election, for example, the average ranking of a candidate was 2.5, exactly the mid-point between the last-winning candidate (i.e., second place) and the first-losing candidate (i.e., third place). Being on a slate reduced a candidate's expected rank ordering by 0.31. In contrast, contending as an independent against a slate increased one's rank ordering by 0.28. The outcomes of contests in which a lone candidate contended against two allied opponents were thus decidedly in favor of the latter. However – and as one might expect – the advantage that running on a slate conferred on a candidate was negligible when his opponents also ran as a slate.

The Institutionalization of Party Slates

We noted earlier that a large majority of slates were one-shot interactions in terms of the individual candidates who comprised them. If slates were merely temporary expedients that allowed two candidates to do well at a given election, then it is hard to accept our interpretation that the rise of party slates was an important stepping stone in the evolution of political parties. This raises the question of whether slates, once they were established in a constituency, tended to fade away with the specific candidates involved or persist at later elections, albeit with different candidates?

The short answer is that once slates were employed in a constituency, they tended to be used subsequently. We show this by regressing a variable that indicates that at least one party's candidates ran as a slate at the elections in constituency j at time t (USEDSLATE$_{jt}$) on a lagged version of the same variable, controlling for constituency fixed effects, i.e.,

$$USEDSLATE_{jt} = \beta_0 + \beta_1 USEDSLATE_{jt-1} + \sum \delta_j D_j + e_{jt} \qquad (4.6)$$

where $\sum \delta_j D_j$ represents the fixed-effect for constituency j. If slates were an institutional development rather than a temporary expedient, we should observe $\beta_1 > 0$. Estimating Equation 4.6 via OLS returns the following estimates:

$$USEDSLATE_{jt} = \underset{(0.01)}{0.30^\dagger} + \underset{(0.03)}{0.18^\dagger} USEDSLATE_{jt-1} + \sum \delta D_j$$

N = 2,404 R^2=0.23

Robust standard errors in parentheses. *p <0.10 **p <0.05 †p <0.01

The coefficient on $USEDSLATE_{jt-1}$ tells us that the probability of a slate being formed by at least one party at an election in a constituency increases by 0.18 if candidates ran as a slate at previous election in the constituency. In that sense, party slates represented an institutional development rather than a temporary expedient. We concede that differences between constituencies account for the bulk of the variation in the data: if we omit $USEDSLATE_{jt-1}$ from the model and regress $USEDSLATE_{jt}$ on a set of constituency fixed effects, we find that the R^2 declines only by 0.02. Thus, cross-constituency variation is 10 times as great as within-constituency variation. This is indicative of the fact that there were constituencies in which elections were always organized and contested along party lines (e.g., Ipswich, Cambridge, and Leicester) and others in which elections were organized and contested along personal and parochial lines.

4.5.3 Alternative Mechanisms

The fundamental nature of the electorate's party orientation is an open question, but it is not one that is critical for us to answer. The decline of split voting tells us that any distinctions that Victorian voters perceived between candidates bearing the same party label were increasingly overshadowed by what they perceived to be more substantial distinctions between candidates bearing different party labels. Whether these distinctions were ideological or affective, or driven by party policy rather than identity, is hard to assess. It was not that Victorian voters were unable to connect their own material interests to the parties' policy positions (e.g., Jaggard 2004; Phillips 1992; Phillips and Wetherell 1995), but rather that in many localities the parties' labels also evoked sectarian identities and customary loyalties (Moore 1976). We also recognize that the electorate's rising party orientation offers one possible explanation as to why copartisan candidates were able to overcome their collective action problem and run as a financially integrated slate. Other mechanisms might also have allowed copartisan candidates to forge party slates, and we consider these alternatives.

Political Culture

One can explain the growing propensity of candidates to contest elections as slates as a function of a changing political culture. Nineteenth-century parliamentary elections took place in the shadow of a long-standing suspicion of political parties (Kishlansky 1986; Scarrow 2006). It was common in the 1830s, but even as late as the 1860s, for candidates to pronounce that they stood independently from any party (Gash 1953; Hanham 1959). There were ideological and organizational aspects to these pronouncements in that candidates would not only declare their intention to judge issues on their merits (rather than on a partisan basis), but also disavow being part of a coalition. Indeed, losing candidates frequently accused the winners of having won the election via a covert and dishonorable coalition. One can thus argue that the growth in party slates was due to the slow dissolution of these antiparty norms. Such an argument is dogged by endogeneity (perhaps expressed norms merely justified existing practices), and it also fails to specify the mechanism by which the customary suspicion of party gave way to a system in which the majority of candidates openly campaigned as members of party slates.

Central Party Direction

An argument that the long-run increase in party slates reflects the growing strength of party organization is on stronger footing, but it must be carefully circumscribed. Party organization cannot be understood as the centralized direction of local campaigns. Prior to the 1870s, the central party organizations (and applying this term is anachronistic) were simply networks of individuals who dispensed information and advice – for example, as to whom local elites might approach to stand as a candidate (Gash 1953; Gash 1983, 133; Jaggard 2008; Newbould 1985). As such, the central parties lacked the capacity to intervene in local affairs. This was particularly the case because local candidates provided the bulk of their own electioneering expenses. It would be similarly anachronistic to ascribe the increase in slates to the organizational force of the party caucuses that Ostrogorski (1902) described; these organizations arrived on the scene only in the late 1860s (Cox 1987) and were not, in any case, always able to dictate who would stand as the constituency's candidate or how the local campaign would be conducted (see, e.g., Owen 2008). The formation of slates preceded both central party organization and party caucuses.

Ideology and Policy

One could argue that the financial free-rider problem declined as the parties became more ideologically cohesive. On this interpretation, the problems that copartisan candidates confronted in forming and maintaining slates were principally due to divisions within each party on various policies – for example, free trade on the Conservative side, electoral reform and Ireland on the Liberal side, etc. As these divisions eased, copartisans ran as slates.

We have already acknowledged that political and electoral considerations influenced the decision to take on a running mate. Our argument is that crucial economic factors also played a role in the formation of party slates. Building party organization was not merely an ideological project; it was also an economic one. Even so, there are difficulties with the argument that party slates were primarily a function of ideological concord within the two parties. The first difficulty is logical. Ideological agreement may be a necessary condition for slates to form, but it is hard to see how it was a sufficient condition because it does not resolve the financial free-rider problem. The second difficulty is empirical. The main parties were split on many issues over the course of the century, and party unity in House of Commons divisions reached modern (i.e., high) levels only in 1874 (Eggers and Spirling 2016). Figure 4.1 shows that the move toward party slates was underway well before that time.

The Extension of the Franchise and Registration Societies

Another possibility is that the increase in party slates was an outgrowth of the registration societies that sprang up in the 1830s in response to the First Reform Act. Contemporaries quickly understood that one of the chief effects of the First Reform Act was to place a premium on registration of voters, and local registration societies were constructed to meet this new demand. Salmon (2002) argues that these registration societies were crucial to the mobilization of a party-oriented electorate, and that they were effective progenitors of the local party organizations that would come to monopolize the nomination of candidates and the conduct of local elections.

Again, limits must be placed on any argument that casts registration societies (or related organizations, such as Conservative workingmen's associations or nonconformist friendly societies) as capable of either inducing or compelling candidates of the same party to run as a slate. First, many registration societies lived a tenuous existence that depended heavily on the financial support of a local MP or prospective candidate (Gash 1983). The registration society thus served rather than governed MPs and candidates. Second, such societies sometimes undermined rather than reinforced intraparty unity (e.g., Newbould 1985; Gent 2012). Third, the efforts of an effective registration society would at most produce an electoral register that promised a given party's candidates success at the upcoming election. An inviting register might induce an additional candidate to contest the constituency, but why it would induce those candidates to contest the election as a slate is unclear.

4.6 Conclusion

In the 1830s, the tradition was for candidates of the same party to contest multimember constituencies independently. Losing candidates would frequently denounce their opponents for having contested the election as a coalition; the winners would keenly protest that they had fought the election independently. By the 1860s, however, electoral competition ran mainly along party lines. Copartisans in multi-member constituencies tended to contest the election as a party alliance, so the modal pattern of electoral competition in two-member constituencies consisted of a slate of two Liberals contending against a slate of two Conservatives.

Contesting an election as a coalition offered candidates financial and electoral benefits. The corresponding difficulty was that each copartisan worried that his financial contribution would work mainly to get his running mate elected. The rise of a party-oriented electorate resolved this financial free-riding problem: once voters cast their votes on the basis of party labels, each candidate could be confident that a vote for his copartisan running mate would be accompanied by a vote for himself. Once one side succeeded in forming a coalition, competitive pressures led the other side to follow suit, and once coalitions took hold in a constituency, they tended to persist.

Change thus proceeded on three dimensions: the modal number of candidates contesting two-member constituencies increased from three to four, three-cornered contests gave way to bipartisan competition between party slates, and the nature of electoral competition evolved from personal to partisan. The formation of party alliances was an important step in this process because it simultaneously imparted a bipartisan uniformity to the structure of constituency-level competition at British parliamentary elections and subordinated the individual candidate to the party label (Ostrogorski 1902). These developments in turn facilitated the development of nationalized and programmatic electoral competition (Caramani 2003; Cox 1987).

5 Conclusion

5.1 Summary and Conclusions

On hearing of Palmerston's death, Disraeli remarked that "the truce of the parties is now over" (Briggs 1972, 227). Our analysis suggests that it ended months earlier, at the 1865 general election, and perhaps as early as 1859. From 1859 onward the proportion of elections being contested by candidates of both parties grew rapidly. Two factors were critical to the spread of electoral contestation. First, socioeconomic changes ensured that by the 1870s there were few constituencies that were so structurally biased against one party as to preclude electoral competition. Institutional changes, such as the redistribution of 1868, contributed to this process, but it was mainly a function of industrialization and urbanization. Second, literacy and the spread of newspapers made it easier for candidates to engage and mobilize their supporters. At least, we infer this from the correlation between literacy and electoral contestation, and the fact that contestation surged just after the removal of the stamp duty in 1855 and did so in the constituencies where newspaper penetration was deepest. Our general conclusion on this front – that electoral contestation emerged as electoral strongholds gave way to electoral battlegrounds – is similar to Caramani's, but we provide insights into the mechanisms that drove this process.

Elections were not only contested more frequently than they had been in the pre-Reform era, they also became more expensive to contest. Even as the cost of electioneering increased, however, the marginal effect of money on votes declined. This result connects our work to that of Camp et al. (2014), who point to the decline in the marginal value of election agents to candidates as one reason for the demise of electoral corruption after the 1880s. We agree that the marginal value of electoral corruption declined, but it did not fall to zero and the prize – a seat in the House of Commons – remained valuable enough to sustain electoral corruption.

Candidates adapted to these changing conditions by forming slates. A slate allowed copartisans to split the fixed costs of fighting the election, giving them a spending advantage over candidates who continued to run independently. One consequence of this organizational change was that elections in multimember constituencies were increasingly swept by members of the same party rather than being split between candidates of the two parties. Thus, just as strongholds gave way to battlegrounds, splits gave way to sweeps. These trends were amplified by the extension of the suffrage in 1868, but they began before 1868 and were rooted in the resumption of two-party competition in the late 1850s and the rise of a party-oriented electorate. Our inference on this front – that the electorate's rising party orientation was critical to the emergence of elections as moments of national and partisan competition – dovetails with Cox's (1987) argument, but again, by showing the link between party orientation and slate formation, we provide insights into the mechanisms underlying these changes.

Our account of the evolution of the economic basis of electioneering between 1832 and 1880 raises questions about change and continuity. Why did candidates generally observe the complex and stringent regulations of the 1883

Corrupt and Illegal Practices Act when they had so widely disregarded the less onerous rules of the 1854 Corrupt Practices Act? If the probability and cost of fighting a contested election increased so rapidly in the short span of time between 1859 and 1868, why did candidates and parties not more quickly shift away from the traditional electoral strategies of bribery, treating, and fictitious employment and adopt more cost-effective programmatic electoral strategies?

The answer to why candidates disregarded the 1854 Corrupt Practices Act strikes us as straightforward. Up until 1859, the marginal effect of money on votes was significant; a spending advantage over one's opponents of even £200 was sufficient to win a large proportion of elections. Furthermore, while electioneering in this fashion was expensive, two factors kept the expense manageable. First, electorates were small. Second, the probability of an uncontested election remained high. The first factor applied mainly to the boroughs; the second mainly to the counties. In either case, however, the benefits of fighting elections via clientelism exceeded the associated costs.

By 1868, the marginal effect of money on votes had declined even as the extension of the suffrage and the spread of electoral contestation had substantially increased electioneering costs. We see three reasons why it took three more elections and a further extension of the suffrage to induce parties and candidates to adopt more cost-effective programmatic electoral strategies. First, while the expected cost of an election rose substantially from £800 in 1859 to £1,300 in 1868, a large proportion of candidates were wealthy enough to afford this increase. Second, the rate at which candidates petitioned elections and the amounts that they spent on those petitions indicates that candidates continued to place a sufficiently high value on a parliamentary seat to justify the increase in electioneering costs. Third, candidates in multimember constituencies were able to form coalitions with their copartisans. Coalitions lowered candidate's individual expenses by 15–25 percent (see Table 4.2) and provided them with a significant spending advantage over singleton opponents. Of course, candidates who contested single-member constituencies could not take financial shelter in a coalition, but the single-member constituencies that were left in place by the Second Reform Act were not large, with a median electorate of just 1,400.

The reforms of 1884 and 1885 were far more extensive than those of 1868. The extension of the franchise increased the electorate from three to five million, and it grew quickly thereafter. Had elections continued to be conducted on a clientelistic basis, the extension of the franchise in 1884 would have increased electioneering costs by 20 percent relative to 1880. This estimate is a conservative one: it does not account for two additional factors. First, the proportion of contested elections was 10 percent higher in 1885 than in 1880. Second, it does not account for the near-abolition of multi-member constituencies. The effect of this was that the vast majority of candidates had to bear single-handedly the overhead costs of mounting an election campaign, and they had to do so in single-member constituencies that were much larger than the single-member constituencies that existed between 1868 and 1880. We agree with Chadwick (1976) and Rix (2016) as to the importance of the reforms of 1884 and 1885.

Once the electoral system reached the tipping point of 1885, candidates and parties overhauled their electoral strategies and their organizations. The Liberal central party organization distributed £87,910 to candidates at the 1906 election, and the Conservative Central Office distributed £100,000 to candidates at the 1910 election (Rix 2016, 196–197). These funds were accompanied by a massive volume of printed material that was produced and distributed by the central parties for use by candidates and local parties. This was a complete reversal of the state of affairs that had prevailed up to 1860. The central parties in the 1840s, for example, dispersed less £15,000 per election (see, e.g., Gash 1953; Gash 1983; Gwynn 1962; Pinto-Dushinsky 1981) and produced no literature whatsoever. At the constituency level, candidates at elections from 1885 onward relied on volunteer associations as substitutes for the cash that their predecessors had previously used to fight elections. In the space of twenty years, the two main parties transformed from coteries of local notables who employed clientelism to win elections to electoral-professional parties that fought elections on the basis of volunteers and policies. All of these later developments, however, followed a surge in contested elections and party slates that began in earnest in 1865. Party slates ensured that elections ran along clear two-party lines, imparting a coherence and consistency to party labels across constituencies. This, in turn, made it easier for parties to execute programmatic campaign strategies – although it is more accurate to state the matter in the contrapositive: absent competitive elections run along stable partisan lines, programmatic electoral politics would not have emerged.

We titled this Element *The Economic Origins of Political Parties*, and there are two reasons for this. First, our analyses show that candidates' behavior was often motivated by economic concerns. Money was both the problem and, in some ways, the solution, in that its declining capacity to alter election outcomes spurred changes that were not forthcoming in response to legislative efforts. Second, it provides a way to think about the behavior of candidates and parties that is motivated by and consistent with what we know from a variety of contexts. For example, drawing an economic analogy between candidates and firms competing in an industry, we might say that in the face of increased competition and higher costs, candidates preferred to eke out efficiencies by consolidating with copartisans rather than by changing technology. It took an additional shock to market conditions (in the form of an even more extensive expansion of the franchise and a wholesale redistribution of parliamentary seats and constituency boundaries) to convince candidates and parties to adopt an altogether different business model. The second point is particularly important as it leads to questions about the broader relevance of our analyses. Was what happened in Victorian England sui generis, or are there general lessons that apply elsewhere? We answer this question by comparing the elections of modern India to those of Victorian England.

5.2 Implications and Relevance: A Comparison to Modern India

The similarities between the elections in Victorian England and those in present-day India are manifest. In both cases, we observe candidates relying on the provision of food, drink, jobs, and money to win elections. The result in both cases is tremendously expensive election campaigns that require candidates to secure large amounts of illicit money (Banyan 2014; Bussell 2018; Sen 2009). Just as in Victorian England, Indian politicians and voters share the belief that electoral corruption, while perhaps regrettable, is unavoidable and morally acceptable (Sen 2009, Weschle 2016). As in England, legislative efforts in India to limit election spending and to purify election campaigns are largely unsuccessful and widely ignored (Gowda and Sridharan 2012).

The high cost of elections had similar effects on parties. A customary attachment to local autonomy inclined the two main British parties to leave matters of candidate selection, fund raising, and electoral tactics to local notables. As we have stressed, however, the central parties had little capacity to do otherwise: they lacked the organizational and economic power to direct local campaigns, and they were heavily reliant on candidates to pay their own electioneering expenses. This imbalance in financial resources helped to ensure that elections in many constituencies remained personal and parochial affairs. The reliance on "black money" to fund election campaigns has had a similar effect on Indian parties. Criminals – who have ready access to such illicit funds – are increasingly attractive candidates, and they are sometimes able to simply buy their nominations from the parties (Vaishnav 2012). The parties themselves have increasingly become personal and dynastic vehicles (Chhibber 2013), with the attendant consequence that elections are personalistic and sectarian rather than programmatic. The result in both cases is a parliamentary plutocracy, where many MPs are multimillionaires (Sen 2009; Vaishnav 2012; Fisman et al. 2014).

There also exists a similarity between our work and Wilkinson's (2007) three-stage model of Indian political development. Wilkinson breaks down the evolution of electoral competition in India into three eras. In the first era, just after partition, the Congress party relied on upper-caste local intermediaries to deliver the votes of poor and low-caste voters to the Congress. These upper-caste local intermediaries did not need to bribe or otherwise entice voters to vote for Congress; they could rely on their social status and economic dominance to cow poor and lower-caste voters to do as they directed. Elections were thus uncompetitive and inexpensive. The internal break-down of the Congress Party in the late 1960s, and the consequent surge in electoral competition, marked the start of a second era. In this second era, elected politicians of all stripes and at all levels of government used their offices to extort the business and agricultural sectors, to enrich themselves certainly, but mainly to fight increasingly expensive elections. In this era, political graft, patronage, and electoral corruption increased in lockstep. India is now, Wilkinson argues, "at the beginning of a third era, in which the costs of clientelism in India are increasing and unsustainable, and the political constituency in favor of political reform of the existing patron–client structures is growing in size and political importance" (Wilkinson 2007, 112).

In one sense, our work on the political economy of elections in Victorian England supports Wilkinson's optimism. Wilkinson's three eras parallel our depiction of England's path out of an uncompetitive era, via a second era of electoral competition and clientelism, to a third era in which candidates and parties responded to the declining efficiency and increasing costs of clientelism by altering their electoral organizations and strategies. That said, our work also stresses the "stickiness" of institutional practices and beliefs: that as long as politicians believe that money is critical to winning elections, they will resist institutional incentives to fight elections cleanly. In turn, the comparison between Victorian England and modern India highlights the implicit limitations of our argument. Indian elections have all the institutional trappings of modern democracy: a universal franchise on the world's most massive scale, a secret ballot, legal limits of campaign spending, and political parties. Even so, Indian elections remain exceedingly corrupt and many parties are merely personal vehicles. The Indian example thus underscores the fact that the changes in electoral contestation, the extension of the suffrage, and the economics and organization of election campaigns were at most necessary conditions for the emergence of nationalized and programmatic electoral competition in England and Wales.

5.3 Final Words

We posed two questions at the outset of this study: (1) what made candidates increasingly willing to contest parliamentary elections, and (2) what induced them to contest elections as a party standard bearers? Our answer to the first question is that socioeconomic changes made it viable for Liberal candidates to contest constituencies that they had previously found to be unwinnable. The spread of literacy and the rise of cheap newspapers accelerated these trends. Our answer to the second question is that the economic pressures generated by frequent electoral contestation in larger constituencies induced copartisan candidates to contest elections as slates. This imparted a uniform partisan character to parliamentary elections that facilitated the emergence of programmatic politics.

Bibliography

Adelman, Paul (1989). *Peel and the Conservative Party 1830–1850*. London and New York: Longman.

Aldrich, John H. (1995). *Why Parties? The Origin and Transformation of Parties in America*. Chicago: University of Chicago Press.

Aydelotte, William O. (1966). "Parties and Issues in Early Victorian England." *Journal of British Studies* 5(2): 95–114.

Banyan (2014). "Campaign Finance in India: Black Money Power." *The Economist*, 4 May.

Braggion, Fabio and Lyndon Moore (2013). "The Economic Benefits of Political Connections in Late Victorian Britain." *Journal of Economic History* 73(1): 142–176.

Briggs, Asa (1972). *Victorian People: A Reassessment of Persons and Themes 1851–67*. Chicago: University of Chicago Press.

Bussell, Jennifer (2018). *Costs of Democracy: Political Finance in India*. Oxford: Oxford University Press.

Camp, Edwin, Avinash Dixit, and Susan Stokes (2014). "Catalyst or Cause? Legislation and the Demise of Machine Politics in Britain and the United States." *Legislative Studies Quarterly* 39(4): 559–592.

Caramani, Daniele (2003). "The End of Silent Elections: The Birth of Electoral Competition, 1832–1915." *Party Politics* 9(4): 411–443.

Caramani, Daniele (2004). *The Nationalization of Politics: The Formation of National Electorates and Party Systems in Western Europe*. Cambridge and New York: Cambridge University Press.

Chadwick, Mary E. J. (1976). "The role of Redistribution in the Making of the Third Reform Act." *The Historical Journal* 19(September): 665–683.

Chhibber, Pradeep (2013). "Dynastic parties: Organization, finance and impact." *Party Politics* 19(2): 277–295.

Chhibber, Pradeep and Kenneth Kollman (2004). *The Formation of National Party Systems: Federalism and Party Competition in Canada, Great Britain, India, and the United States*. Princeton: Princeton University Press.

Chilcott, J. V. (1837). *An Alphabetical List of the Poll Taken at the General Election of Members to Serve in Parliament for the Borough of Leominster*. Leominster, 24 July.

Cipolla, Carlo M. (1969). *Literacy and Development in the West*. New York: Penguin.

Coates, R. Morris and Thomas R. Dalton (1992). "Entry Barriers in Politics and Uncontested Elections." *Journal of Political Economy* 49(1): 75–90.

Conacher, James B. (1972). *The Peelites and the Party System, 1846–52.* Newton Abbot: David & Charles.

Coppedge, Michael (1997). "Modernization and Thresholds of Democracy: Evidence for a Common Path and Process." In Manus I. Midlarsky (Ed.), *Inequality, Democracy, and Economic Development.* Cambridge and New York: Cambridge University Press.

Cox, Gary W. (1987). *The Efficient Secret: The Cabinet and the Development of Political Parties in Victorian England.* Cambridge and New York: Cambridge University Press.

Cox, Gary W. (1997). *Making Votes Count: Strategic Coordination in the World's Electoral Systems.* Cambridge and New York: Cambridge University Press.

Craig, F. W. S. (1977). *British Parliamentary Election Results, 1832–1880.* London and Basingstoke: Macmillan.

Dahl, R. A. (1973). *Polyarchy: Participation and Opposition.* New Haven: Yale University Press.

Downs, Anthony (1957). *An Economic Theory of Political Action in a Democracy.* Chicago: University of Chicago Press.

Duverger, Maurice (1962). *Political Parties.* Barbara North and Robert North (Trans.). New York: Wiley.

Eggers, Andrew C. and Arthur Spirling (2016). "Party Cohesion in Westminster Systems: Inducements, Replacement and Discipline in the House of Commons, 1836–1910." *British Journal of Political Science* 46(3): 567–589.

Fisman, R., F. Schulz, and V. Vig (2014). "The Private Returns to Public Office." *Journal of Political Economy* 122(4): 806–862.

Gash, Norman (1953). *Politics in the Age of Peel: A Study in the Technique of Parliamentary Representation.* Atlantic Highlands: Harvester Press.

Gash, Norman (1983). "The Organization of the Conservative Party 1832–1846: Part II: The Electoral Organization." *Parliamentary History* 2 (January): 131–152.

Gent, David (2012): "The Politics of Disinterest: The Whigs and the Liberal Party in the West Riding of Yorkshire, 1830–1850." *Northern History* 49(2): 302–322.

Gowda M. V. R. and E. Sridharan (2012). "Reforming India's Party Financing and Election Expenditure Laws." *Election Law Journal* 11(2): 226–240.

Great Britain. General Register Office. (1837). Annual report of the Registrar-General of births, deaths and marriages in England. London: Printed by W. Clowes and Sons for H.M.S.O.

Green, Donald P. and Jonathan S. Krasno (1988). "Salvation for the Spendthrift Incumbent: Reestimating the Effects of Campaign Spending in House Elections." *American Journal of Political Science* 32(4): 884–907.

Gurowich, P. M. (1984). "The Continuation of War by Other Means: Party and Politics, 1855–1865." *The Historical Journal* 27(3): 603–631.

Gwyn, William (1962). *Democracy and the Cost of Politics in Britain*. London: Athlone Press.

Hanham, H. J. (1959). *Elections and Party Management: Politics in the Time of Disraeli and Gladstone*. London and New York: Longmans.

Hicken, Allen (2009). *Building Party Systems in Developing Democracies*. Cambridge and New York: Cambridge University Press.

Jacobson, Gary C. (1990). "The Effect of Campaign Spending in House Elections: New Evidence for Old Arguments." *American Journal of Political Science* 34(2): 334–362.

Jaggard, Edwin (2004). "Small Town Politics in Mid-Victorian Britain." *History* 89(293): 2–29.

Jaggard, Edwin (2008). "Managers and Agents: Conservative Party Organisation in the 1850s." *Parliamentary History* 27(1): 7–18.

Kam, Christopher (2009). *Party Discipline and Parliamentary Government*. Cambridge and New York: Cambridge University Press.

Kam, Christopher (2017). "The Secret Ballot and the Market for Votes at 19th-Century British Elections." *Comparative Political Studies* 50(5): 594–635.

Key, V. O. (1949). *Southern Politics*. New York: Alfred A. Knopf.

Kishlansky, Mark (1986). *Parliamentary Selection: Social and Political Choice in Early Modern England*. Cambridge and New York: Cambridge University Press.

Kitschelt, Herbert and Steven I. Wilkinson (2007). "Citizen–Politician Linkages: An Introduction." In Herbert Kitschelt and Steven I. Wilkinson (Eds.), *Patrons, Clients, and Policies: Patterns of Democratic Accountability and Political Competition*. Cambridge and New York: Cambridge University Press.

Kuo, Didi (2018). *Clientelism, Capitalism, and Democracy: The Rise of Programmatic Politics in the United States and Britain*. Cambridge and New York: Cambridge University Press.

LaPalombara, Joseph and Myron Weiner (1966). *Political Parties and Political Development*. Princeton University Press.

Lee, Alan J. (1976). *The Origins of the Popular Press in England, 1855–1914*. London and Basingstoke: Taylor and Francis.

Lerner, Daniel (1958). *The Passing of Traditional Society*. Glencoe: The Free Press.

Levitt, Steven D. (1994). "Using Repeat Challengers to Estimate the Effect of Campaign Spending on Election Outcomes in the US House." *Journal of Political Economy* 102(4): 777–798.

Lijphart, Arend (1994). *Electoral Systems and Party Systems*. Oxford: Oxford University Press.

Lipset, Seymour Martin (1959). "Some Social Requisites of Democracy: Economic Development and Political Legitimacy." *American Political Science Review* 53(1): 69–105.

Lipset, Seymour Martin and Stein Rokkan (1967). "Cleavage Structures, Party Systems, and Voter Alignments: An Introduction." In Seymour Martin Lipset and Stein Rokkan (Eds.), *Party Systems and Voter Alignments: Cross-National Perspectives*. New York: Free Press.

Lloyd, Trevor (1965). "Uncontested Seats in British General Elections, 1852–1910." *The Historical Journal* 8(2): 260–265.

Manin, Bernard (1997). *The Principles of Representative Government*. Cambridge and New York: Cambridge University Press.

Mares, Isabela and Boliang Zhu (2015). "The Production of Electoral Intimidation: Economic and Political Incentives." *Comparative Politics* 48(1): 23–43.

McLean, Iain (2001) *Rational Choice and British Politics: An Analysis of Rhetoric and Manipulation from Peel to Blair*. Oxford: Oxford University Press.

Mitch, David (1992) *The Rise of Popular Literacy in Victorian England: The Influence of Private Choice and Public Policy*. Philadelphia: University of Pennsylvania Press.

Moore, D. C. (1976). *The Politics of Deference: A Study of the Mid-Nineteenth Century English Political System*. Hassocks: Harvester Press.

Musson, Alfred Edward (1958). "Newspaper Printing in the Industrial Revolution." *The Economic History Review* 10(3): 411–426.

Newbould, Ian (1985). "Whiggery and the Growth of Party 1830–41: Organization and the Challenge of Reform." *Political History* 4(1): 137–156.

Noble, John Jr. (1859). *Poll Book of the Contested Election of the Borough of Boston*. April 30.

O'Gorman, Frank (1984). "Electoral Deference in 'Unreformed' England: 1760–1832." *Journal of Modern History* 56(3): 391–429.

O'Leary, Cornelius (1962). *The Elimination of Corrupt Practices in British Elections, 1868–1911*. Oxford: Clarendon.

Ostrogorski, Mosei (1902). *Democracy and the Organization of Political Parties*, Volume I (1964 Edition). Garden City: Doubleday & Co.

Owen, James (2008). "Triangular Contests and Caucus Rhetoric at the 1885 General Elections." *Parliamentary History* 27(2): 215–235.

Philbin, J. Holladay (1965). *Parliamentary Representation, 1832 England and Wales*. New Haven: Yale University Press.

Phillips, John A. (1992). *The Great Reform Bill in the Boroughs: English Electoral Behaviour, 1818–1841*. Oxford: Oxford University Press.

Phillips, John A. and Charles Wetherell (1995). "The Great Reform Bill of 1832 and the Political Modernization of England." *American Historical Review* 100(2): 411–436.

Pinto-Dushinsky, Michael (1981). *British Political Finance*. Washington, DC and London: American Enterprise Institution for Public Policy Research.

Przeworski, Adam, Susan C. Stokes, and Bernard Manin (1999). "Elections and Representation." In Adam Przeworski, Susan C. Stokes, and Bernard Manin (Eds.), *Democracy, Accountability, and Representation*. Cambridge and New York: Cambridge University Press.

Putnam, R., D. R. Leonardi, and R. Y. Nanetti (1994) *Making Democracy Work: Civic Traditions in Modern Italy*. Princeton: Princeton University Press.

Rix, Kathryn (2016). *Parties, Agents, and Electoral Culture in England, 1880–1910*. Rochester: Boydell Press.

Rubinstein, William D. (1981). *Men of Property: The Very Wealthy in Britain since the Industrial Revolution*. London and New York: Taylor and Francis.

Rubinstein, William D. (1983). "The End of 'Old Corruption' in Britain 1780–1860." *Past & Present* 10(1): 55–86.

Rueschemeyer, D., E. H. Stephens, and J. D. Stephens (1992). *Capitalist Development and Democracy*. Chicago: University of Chicago Press.

Salmon, Philip J. (2002). *Electoral Reform at Work: Local Politics and National Parties, 1832–1841*. Woodbridge and Rochester: Boydell Press for the Royal Historical Society.

Scarrow, Susan E. (2006). "The Nineteenth-century Origins of Modern Political Parties: The Unwanted Emergence of Party-based Politics." In Richard S. Katz and William J. Crotty (Eds.), *Handbook of Party Politics*. Thousand Oaks: Sage.

Schlesinger, Joseph A. (1984). "On the Theory of Party Organization." *The Journal of Politics* 46(2): 369–400.

Sen, R. (2009). "India's 2009 Elections: The Problem of Corruption." *Journal of Democracy* 20(4): 89–92.

Seymour, Charles (1915). *Electoral Reform in England and Wales: The Development and Operation of the Parliamentary Franchise, 1832–1885*. New Haven: Yale University Press.

Simpson, Miles (1997). "Informational Inequality and Democracy in the New World Order." In Manus I. Midlarsky (Ed.), *Inequality, Democracy, and Economic Development*. Cambridge and New York: Cambridge University Press.

Stokes, Susan C., Thad Dunning, Marcelo Nazareno, and Valeria Brusco (2013). *Brokers, Voters, and Clientelism: The Puzzle of Distributive Politics*. Cambridge and New York: Cambridge University Press.

Stone, Lawrence (1969). "Literacy and Education in England 1640–1900." *Past & Present* 42(1): 69–139.

Taagepera, Rein and Matthew Soberg Shugart (1989) *Seats and Votes: The Effects and Determinants of Electoral Systems*. New Haven: Yale University Press.

Teorell, Jan (2010). *Determinants of Democratization: Explaining Regime Change in the World, 1972–2006*. Cambridge and New York: Cambridge University Press.

Thomas, Alun J. (1950). "The System of Registration and the Development of Party Organisation, 1832–1870." *History* 35(123–124): 81–98.

Tocqueville, Alexis de (2000) *Democracy in America*, Volumes I and II (1935 Edition) Henry Reeve (Trans.). New York: Bantam.

Vaishnav, Milan (2012). *The Merits of Money and "Muscle": Essays on Criminality, Elections and Democracy in India*. PhD Dissertation, Columbia University.

Vanhanen, Tatu (2004). *Democratization: A Comparative Analysis of 170 Countries*. London and New York: Routledge.

Vincent, J. R. (1966). *The Formation of the British Liberal Party*. New York: Scribner.

Weedon, Alexis (2003). *Victorian Publishing: The Economics of Book Production for a Mass Market*. Aldershot: Ashgate.

Weschle, S. (2016). "Punishing Personal and Electoral Corruption: Experimental Evidence from India", *Research & Politics* 3(2): https://doi .org/10.1177/2053168016645136.

Wilkinson, Steven I. (2007). "Explaining Changing Patterns of Voter–Party Linkages in India." In Herbert Kitschelt and Steven I. Wilkinson (Eds.), *Patrons, Clients, and Policies: Patterns of Democratic Accountability and Political Competition*. Cambridge and New York: Cambridge University Press.

Ziblatt, Daniel (2017). *Conservative Political Parties and the Birth of Modern Democracy in Europe*. Cambridge and New York: Cambridge University Press.

Acknowledgments

Thanks to Ken Carty, Ben Nyblade, Alberto Simpser, Scott Desposato, Anjali Bohlken, participants at the UBC Department of Economics Empirical Workshop Seminar, and participants at the LSE Conference on Historical Institutions for their helpful comments; to Benjamin Miller, Robert Schwarz, David Mitch, Patrick Kuhn and Nick Vivyan; and to the History of Parliament Trust for sharing data. Funding for this work was provided by the Hampton Fund of the University of British Columbia and the Social Sciences and Humanities Council of Canada.

Cambridge Elements ☰

Political Economy

David Stasavage
New York University

David Stasavage is Julius Silver Professor in the Wilf Family Department of Politics at New York University. He previously held positions at the London School of Economics and at Oxford University. His work has spanned a number of different fields and currently focuses on two areas: development of state institutions over the long run and the politics of inequality. He is a member of the American Academy of Arts and Sciences.

About the Series

The Element Series Political Economy provides authoritative contributions on important topics in the rapidly growing field of political economy. Elements are designed so as to provide broad and in depth coverage combined with original insights from scholars in political science, economics, and economic history. Contributions are welcome on any topic within this field.

Cambridge Elements ☰

Political Economy

Elements in the Series